OPEN THE DOORS

OF THE TEMPLE

THE SURVIVAL OF CHRISTIAN SCIENCE
IN THE
TWENTY-FIRST CENTURY

Nancy Niblack Baxter

Hawthorne Publishing
Carmel, Indiana

ISBN: 0-9726273-1-6

Hawthorne Publishing
15601 Oak Road
Carmel, Indiana 46033

Dedicated to all the bright and eager people who are filling the pews of our church now and who aren't able to join it.

And once again the scene was changed,
New earth there seemed to be
I saw the Holy City, beside the tideless sea:
The light of God was on its streets, The gates were open wide
And all who would might enter,
And no one was denied.
No need of moon or stars by night, or sun to shine by day.
It was the new Jerusalem that would not pass away.

"The Holy City"
F.E. Weatherly

"Healing physical sickness is the smallest part of Christian Science."
Rudimental Divine Science
Mary Baker Eddy

Table of Contents

Preface

Christian Scientists in America belong to one of the most admirable and interesting Christian denominations in the nation today. It has been over one-hundred twenty years since Mary Baker Eddy set up a new and inspired version of practical Christianity. Our movement has had spectacular spiritual success realized through the building of churches world-wide and the healing and revitalization of hundreds of thousands of individual lives through understanding of the eternal Christ. And yet, we are now a diminishing group, beset by declining membership, church closings and financial challenges.

There are many questions involved in analyzing contemporary Christian Science as a movement; this book attempts to deal with only one. Christian Science is struggling in the heartland, and members of churches which are losing members at a steadily continuing rate, with many churches closing regularly, ask "Why aren't people coming to join us?" This book attempts to answer part of that question in an emphatically straight-forward way. My analysis of the crucial question "why aren't people choosing our path of faith" is a three-fold one involving public relations, changing times, and most importantly, a misunderstanding on the part of the faithful of their leader's original intent for her religion. It is, I admit, a radical perspective.

My views stem from my own experience as an historian and writer about public thought and culture. In addition to my experience as an author and publisher whose special focus is nineteenth century history, I have also been involved in public relations and the transmission of information most of my life, and so I believe my perspective stems from some experience. And lastly, I have been a Christian Scientist for over fifty years and intend to stay where I am.

It is a matter of what we have to offer, as it has been for Christianity for over 2,000 years. We in branch churches of the Mother Church, The First Church of Christ, Scientist in Boston, Massachusetts, are on the firing line. We are living our faith amidst conflicting crosscurrents of public opinion and the proliferation of a variety of choices of Christian churches in the community. Just as they have many options in consumer spending, people have many options when they select a religious faith for their lives and families. We Christian Scientists, carrying the torch of an incomparably wonderful way of life, have not often asked the pertinent question, "What do others think of us?" as we observe our neighbors making choices. I believe that although the path of really honest self-examination is not easily trod, it is one we must take.

I hope this book is a thoughtful, if strong-minded, examination of the Christian Science movement for both Christian Scientists and some non-Christian Scientists, at a watershed time. Not everyone will agree with my bold thesis, but I offer it in a spirit of love and devotion to "our leader and our Lord."

I should add that although this is one person's testimony, it is also just one person's opinion.

I have been detailed about what I see as long-overlooked difficulties preventing growth in the Christian Science movement. I have set the development of the problems as I see them against the historical background of Mrs. Eddy's mission and the development of the church. I believe that unless we can understand, and honestly face and overcome, the problems discussed in this book, we cannot easily survive in the future.

The reader will be aware that this book is not done in the Absolute; the Absolute, after all, has no challenges or problems.

Nancy Niblack Baxter
April, 2004

Chapter One

Living—and Dying—in the Light

Christian Science may die as a religion if the present trends continue. In 1951 there were 3,049 churches/societies; my latest count shows about 1,950. Those who heal through prayer, practitioners, have dropped from 10,503 in the early 1950s to about 1,700 today. All across the heartland and south and in the east, many Christian Science churches have become last man clubs, with a few elderly people still keeping the faith and trying to pay the bills on decaying church facilities.

Does it matter? Certainly it does to those of us who are Christian Scientists. But beyond that, it should matter that one of the most interesting and vibrant contributors to the stream of American religious practice, once numbering close to half a million adherents, might vanish. And, certainly, many people would be sorry to not have the controversial leader, Mary Baker Eddy (like Richard Nixon) to "kick around any more."

The reason for the threatened demise? I do not believe, as many Christian Scientists insist, that we are declining because of rampant evil beliefs directed against us, or the world's materialism, or even the continuing factionalism within the ranks of the faithful.

There are, instead, several rather down-to-earth reasons for the decline of Christian Science in the heartland. It is obvious that changing times which have seen the rise of easy and often successful medical solutions to health problems have caused a dramatic change in demand for spiritual healing, and that will be discussed

in Chapter V. But bad press and negative public opinion constitute an even more important reason for "the Great Falling Away."
Closely related to the bad PR, it seems to me, is our own refusal to
understand that the central direction of the movement is astray,
with an emphasis which repels, rather than attracts new adherents.
These are strong charges, but years of observation have shown me
they are true.

Let's begin with the bad press, because it shapes the public
image of who we are. Just as word of mouth sent people to the hill-
sides of Galilee to see "the man who told me everything I ever did,"
word of mouth and its extension, media publicity, can send people
to churches—or away from them. It is not too strong a statement
to say that the movement is being killed by bad PR—but more
importantly, by the regrettable fact that some of that PR is true.

Let's be more specific about that last point. Today, although
many of the things said and printed about Christian Science are
slanderous, ill-researched and downright wrong, and though dis-
affected members have spread malicious gossip which distorts a few
incidents into widespread practice, Christian Scientists themselves
have to take a large share of the blame for what is said about them.

We have not kept up with the trends around us, and the religion we present to the world is unattractive and even frightening, offering in most places little that will draw an adherent who
is expected to change his or her life to join the church.

In an interesting irony, I contend it's not what the founder of
the faith intended, and it can be proven that Mary Baker Eddy
herself came to distrust the phenomenon that is now driving new
converts away and splintering the congregations of the dedicated
remnant, who are very good people with strong dedication to
Christian living.

And what is that phenomenon? The very subject which
should attract those who wish to truly live Christian lives but which
is now the very topic which repels them? It is physical healing,
preached to the exclusion of everything else. There is a culture of
silence within the church, and even among members of branch

churches who are good friends when it comes to do-or-die healing. Nobody in churches I've been active in mentions that we as a denomination are guilty of being a one-note band that no one's listening to. Few in the educational institutions run by Christian Scientists seem to notice that people feel a certain sense of bewilderment or even disgust at our doings—or it seems that way.

The truth is that within the religion I try to practice and love there seems to be a brontosaurus in the living room. Nobody admits to noticing it, and it's about to get up and step on us all. Why don't people come to our public talks in real numbers? Venture into our church sanctuaries to visit? We won't admit it, but people are afraid of us. They believe we let our children sicken and suffer. They say if they join us, "we will have to die if we get too sick." Is that true? If we're honest, we have to admit that it too often is. Because although spiritual healing of the body is one of the great promises and fulfillments of the faith, although it really is one of Jesus' finest gifts to us all and full of realization, too many Christian Scientists don't know what to do when a needed healing is not realized. In every town and city, outsiders watch Christian Scientists sicken and die from illnesses which medical science can now heal fairly easily, and the average person shakes his or her head and wonders.

We've involuntarily come to be bad examples of what might happen when you become a Christian Scientist.

And, saddest of all, those who manage the religion, the higher-ups in the hierarchy, largely downgrade the very crux of this radical religion—that matter is unreal and Spirit is all in the cosmos, this truth which physicists today are reaching towards. The thought-changing Christian core of beliefs the founder articulated are significantly brushed aside in the push towards superficial "get well quick" spirituality, stimulated by the websites run by the church and the misguided idea that people will come into the church seeking spiritual healing over medical care. Some are looking for that, most aren't right now. What they're looking for: a fresh and new form of Christianity to practice every day to transform life and heal the spirit—the reclaiming of identity as children of

God—we can't give because we're fixated on healing the body.

So what we have to give to the religious world is swept right into the corner with the brontosaurus. Overemphasis on spiritual healing—no matter what, do-or-die—is killing us with the world, and I think it is the exact opposite of what Mary Baker Eddy, the founder of the church, intended.

And how did these people find out about our failures and successes in such a public way anyway? The answer is that for over a hundred years newspapers and other media have told them constantly about Christian Science and to this day continue to announce the failures of this religious group they seem to find so fascinating—to our real disadvantage— and have done so since the year of the founding of the faith.

On an April day in 1879, ten students of the Bible met and moved to found a new church. Mary Baker Glover Patterson Eddy, the woman who proposed the motion in that public hall, was a tall, handsome woman with curls bound back by a ribbon and a determined look on her face. She told the group of men and women, who had been meeting as an association in her parlor for some time to hear her give inspiring messages and to read the Bible with them, that her discovery would change the Christian world.

She had hoped not to organize a church, but she had not been able to make much headway with the Christian community in even listening to the discovery she was trying to share: Christianity was actually a provable science whose rules, if humbly and consistently followed, could heal all mankind's ills. Theirs was an age in which science was a by-word; she wanted Christians to view their way as science too. All knew Jesus had accomplished marvelous wonders in His time on earth. He had promised His followers they would do "even greater things" after He was gone, but He did not leave detailed instructions on how the marvels of Christian living were to be accomplished. These Mary believed she had discovered, and she would soon call the detailed description of Jesus' methods of healing mankind Christian Science.

She, and probably her followers, believed that if they founded a church in Boston, the home of intellectual advancement and open-mindedness to change, the truth of Moral Science, as Mrs. Eddy was then calling her religious movement, would be welcomed by the city, and then the nation and world, as a new and practical way of practicing the religion of Jesus.

What they got was not peace, but the sword, at least metaphorically. Christian Science became a hugely successful religious phenomenon in the first four decades of its existence, but it grew to be a world-wide movement only through controversy, skeptical opposition and downright ridicule. That controversy and skepticism troubles the movement even today, when it is a settled denomination languishing in the same slump as mainline Protestant churches—declining congregations and problems of revitalization.

The good news is that the stories of its demise may be premature. The positive, and surprising, story is that Christian Science is beginning to grow again in the heartland with some forward thinkers who are opening wide the windows and letting in the loving and open religion that little group of church founders always hoped for. We have a chance to kick the brontosaurus out the back door, but it will mean a departure from business as usual in the church. But that is ahead of our story.

The roots of the public focus on Christian Science, in periodicals and in the public mind, which so affects the life of our denomination in my view, became vitally important that very first year of formal founding and even before. The intensity and spiritual brilliance of its founder, bordering at times on eccentricity, the predictable inadequacy of its early adherents caused by their own human weaknesses and especially the power of the press, overshadowing everything that happened and transferring it in a distorted fashion to the glass arena of public opinion—all of these thing were present in the 1870, when Mary Baker (then Mrs.

Patterson) called venturesome souls in New England to a new vibrant kind of Christianity.

Some of the early trouble with public perception seems basic to the very process of church founding—at least in the modern world. Establishing a denomination under the glare of nineteenth century media focus was not an easy accomplishment, particularly when the picture was garbled. It is probably only through the lens of time extended over a hundred and twenty years actually, that we can see what the church Mary organized on that day in 1879 was really about. And we may not even be clear about that now.

Founders of denominations never did have it easy. Most were viewed as dangerous lunatics, disturbers of the status quo. They were burned at the stake in England and Bavaria, tossed into dungeons in several places during the Thirty Years War, driven out of the villages of New England. Unless you were part of the group itself, it seemed natural to hate religious denomination founders. Mother Ann of the Shakers got in a ship and sailed for America when she was rejected and persecuted in northern England; then she had to move about in the new nation to keep her people from getting stoned.

But of course not everybody hated the founders of denominations in the sixteenth and seventeenth centuries, because most people didn't even know these founders existed.

The point as it concerns Christian Science is this: the founders and first followers of the earliest denominations, three hundred years ago, existed in shadowy half-light: their beliefs as well as their personal idiosyncrasies spread abroad only by word of mouth, letters and eventually books, which only a few of the learned could read.

By the seventeenth and eighteenth centuries newspapers and books could either present or distort the perceptions of new religious groups—and they did. Witness the strong negative, often derisive comments about John Wesley's odd little group when, after Wesley's heart felt "strangely warmed," he gathered a few students and they first began to meet. These "Methodists" met to practice their methods in the midst of deep controversy and loathing, fanned by the periodicals of the day for those who read. A trend of public examination of religious groups was beginning.

By the late nineteenth century, when Christian Science appeared as a new religious sect, communication had become relatively sophisticated. Most people had access to some sort of periodical; newspapers of one sort or another were available in every hamlet in America, along with books and literate people to read them. Every village of a few hundred people had not one but possibly two newspapers.

And so, when Christian Science began to emerge, it did so in a time of widespread media attention. It also was born in a century when religious devotion did not generally extend to open-mindedness about others' religion. There was a lot of snooping on what people did in their private worship life. A young and lusty America had shown in the 1850s just how narrow-minded and traditional it could be when it dealt with the Mormons by burning their church in Nauvoo eventually and sending the Saints on their way into the uninhabited desert.

These latter-day saints and their teachers (the followers of Joseph Smith and to a much larger degree those of Mrs. Eddy) came into existence in a new era of enhanced literacy and intellectual curiosity among Americans, who had not only been schooled in one-room country schools and academies, but taught to read to expand their horizons. By the 1870s, many had the leisure to think and talk. Libraries were being founded everywhere in the 1880s in small and large towns; lyceum and debating societies drew people out for entertainment. Everybody had an opinion on something or everything. Whatever was going to be done in secret among Christian Scientists was going to be shouted on the mountaintops of Boston or South Bend, Indiana. It was public notice and opinion which built Christian Science (both for better and for worse), just as media focus on some unpleasant truths is helping to destroy it today.

Newspaper articles in Boston in 1879 announced that Mrs.

Eddy and her little group wished to "restore primitive Christianity and its lost element of healing." She was attracting converts because she claimed to have accomplished some astonishing healings on herself and others. The writings she was producing to teach her students the rudiments of the "Moral Science" she was preaching, particularly her new book, were written in complex and convoluted Victorian prose laced throughout with scriptural text. She referred in the book to many familiar names from literature and philosophy. She claimed to have a key to the Scriptures.

The news articles after 1879 said she had finally decided to found a church of "Christ, Scientist" because she believed Jesus taught a way of life which could be practiced and proven as scientific hypotheses are tested and proven. She thought everyday Christians could practice this science themselves if they could learn it, study the Bible and her "textbook." Most radical was her idea that reality is at its essence spiritual, not material. That all men and women were the image and likeness of God, pure and perfect, they just needed to wake up to it. That God intends man, his beloved child, to have dominion over every adverse circumstance—all sin, sickness and even death itself. Forget the Puritans' gloomy predestination and the rigid, joyless orthodoxy of most churches, which emphasized God as punisher and enforcer. The God Christian Science taught was universal Love. That could not help but be attractive, particularly in dour New England. Everyone wished to read about it, to talk about it.

Christian Science spread rapidly in the early days, and the press at that point was a necessary part of the process—a necessary evil, perhaps. Mrs. Eddy began to preach in the large temples of Boston and elsewhere, and word spread that she was an eloquent speaker and that her new, radical ideas made sense. How could such a "different," avant-garde version of Christianity, which emphasized the "nothingness" of matter (and the allness of God) and the necessity to practice the religion in the realm of physical healing as well as daily life find so many adherents? Who were they? Everybody was interested to know that too, and newspapers in Chicago and Philadelphia had personal interviews with new converts to Mrs. Eddy's group.

Early Christian Scientists were middle or upper income men and women who had been brought up in Bible-reading and church-going homes. Many of them, it appears, sincerely wished to look for a "deeper" version of the Christian teaching than they had grown up with; teachings they considered perfunctory or doctrinaire. The sectarianism of the day, much more widespread than we know it today, had disillusioned many churchgoers and they seemed to wish for a purer, joyous version of practical religion. Christian Science held itself out as this purer version of Christ's teachings.

Today, when the press notices religion at all, it usually focuses on religion's ills—the Catholic priests' penchant for young boys, the "religious right's" meddling in politics, the Orthodox Jews in New York and elsewhere defending their rights with violence. And, of course, the Radical Muslims' espousal of killing the infidels to honor Allah. If it's weird, offbeat or negative and connected to religion, it's a story.

In the nineteenth century differences in theology mattered and seemed to be dissected often and publicly in the press as well as at the lectern. Letters-to-the-editor of New England papers debated abstruse religious subjects, explored Biblical passages and told religious stories and jokes. Everybody cared deeply. In the 1870s, when Mary had first begun to invite students to come with her to learn of the "Science of Life" and meet for informal church services, she was making her call to an America fairly saturated with public religious sensibility. Church-going was an integral part of the socializing process of small and large towns; it was a vehicle for meeting people after a busy week on isolated farms; it was a chaste and acceptable way for young people to get together. And it taught the moral lessons the westward-reaching society of post Civil War United States needed to oil the wheels of business growth (not that everyone learned those lessons in the Gilded Age).

It has been estimated that eighty percent of the American population in the 1870s had been brought up in some Christian denomination. They had grown up reading the Bible and understanding it. One need only look at what was considered "light" reading for the Civil War generation to see how many readers (especially women) focused on abstract theological arguments, complex parsing of scriptural texts and especially detailed instructions about how to live the Christian life, day by day and hour by hour. They were in ladies' magazines, along with tips on cooking, sewing fashionable clothing, child-rearing and leisure time activities.

Ladies' books, too, were dominated by Christian religious instruction. A popular book in frontier villages was called *The Angel Visitor*, a sort of series of parables about angels visiting those mourning loved ones taken by the frequent and early death which plagued the times. Included are poems such as:

Lilie Sleeps

And loving hands have brought sweet flowers to strew
Around the couch where little Lilie lies;
Here are fair buds yet moist with morning dew,
And blossoms blushing with celestial dyes
And Lilie sleeps—mar not her peaceful rest,
God knows best.

The reverence and sanctity (or sanctimoniousness) of a good share of the public in the 1860s and 70s does not imply that everybody was that way, of course. On the frontier and many other places irreverence, mockery of religion, atheism and indifference were obvious, as was religious intolerance. And that, too, was spread abroad by the periodicals of the day.

Clearly the reading about religion did not imply tolerance, and that was to be important for the emerging sect known as Christian Science. We can infer from reading the things they read that in this supposedly Christian nation anything radical and new in the way of either politics or religion was suspect. The communal sense of tolerance we have at least attempted to cultivate since the end of the era of the Ku Klux Klan in the Midwest (from 1880 through the 1920s) and the age of social reform came in, was not always a part of the moral ethos in post-Civil War America. Feelings had run deep, fires of distrust and hatred stoked high during the struggle between Northerners and Southerners. People were praised for strength of mind for condemning on the podiums and in newspapers Masons, Catholics, newly freed Blacks, Jews, Europeans, Japanese, Chinese—anybody who was different. Whenever a new church group appeared, it felt picked on and then, when it began to be established, it picked on other, newer groups. And picking on Christian Science became a way of life, for both media sources and those who gained information from them. Christian Science was certainly fair game. It was the element of wonder at the novelty, of oddness, even, of the new religious group, which dominated the first reports, but the reports were also tinged with veiled disapproval.

Even though New England considered itself more broad-minded than everyplace else—after all it had been one of the strongholds of abolitionism and some women were getting together to set agendas for women's rights—it could be quite stiff-necked when religious iconoclasm was concerned. So exact specifics of church dogma, too, were an issue—particularly as Christian Scientists burst upon the scene of the Gilded Age in New England. What was a group's view of Holy Communion? (The Christian Scientists didn't drink actual wine or eat bread—they knelt in their pews to "commune with God" spiritually, without material symbols.) Shocking! And what was this about the Doctrine of Atonement? Reverend Mary Baker Eddy was preaching in her textbook that Atonement should be read at-one-ment—that of course Jesus went to the Cross to save us all but not exactly because he was a sacrificial lamb. He did it so it could bring God and man together through his loving example—to make the world One with its maker. Letters to the editor examined these views (not considered odd today and often accepted by mainline Protestant denominations). News stories attempted to compare, often fairly, just as often not, the new theological beliefs of the days and their relationship to old, time-honored denominational beliefs.

Then there was the personal element. The press of the time sought out celebrity with as much ferocious intensity as it does today, perhaps more. Feature-story writing was coming into its own by the 1890s—personalized stories which featured people and their interests. Reporters sought out sensational happenings, went on trips around the world, visited missionaries in darkest Africa, nosed into many areas which were none of their business, and published their own highly colored versions of the truth for all to read.

And religious leaders were hot topics. Who were these people who seemed to think themselves better than the rest of us? Where do they come from? Can't we discover feet of clay if we dig around enough? From the first moment Mrs. Eddy began to talk about a new kind of religious thinking, the papers were interested in her. She herself sought them out and was a contributor to newspapers of the day.

There was, as a matter of fact, more good press than bad in the process that built Christian Science. In small to medium-sized cities and towns, in larger cities like Chicago, long articles appeared every two or three weeks in the 1880s and 90s describing the charismatic preaching this unusual and beautiful woman was doing, the many who thronged to hear her, the changes in life that they ascribed to her teachings based on a new, modern interpretation of Christianity. This church taught healing as a major premise of its theology. Many there were who flocked to take advantage of that. The papers soon began to pick up the topic of phenomenal growth: this new religion wasn't going to be limited to just one church in Boston. First church in the town, then Second, then Third, sprang up in major cities and mid-sized towns as hundreds and thousands of people latched onto the new form of the Christian religion they'd been brought up with. So *The New York Times*, *The Indianapolis Journal* and *The Star*, *The Chicago Tribune* and *The San Francisco Chronicle* said.

But the bad press was more interesting. This was the age when the very term "Yellow Journalism" evolved, evoking the comic strip character the Yellow Kid. The sensational, the bizarre, the far-out as seen in the public eye became daily fare.

As years went along, in the late nineteenth and early twentieth centuries Christian Scientists were often depicted in the press in different papers or on different days as a weird sect, worshipping a crazy old lady who was much too pushy for her own good, who had a checkered past that many of her old small-town neighbors attested to. She had abandoned her child, so her old neighbors alleged, and was much too uppity. And in later years she was a rich recluse controlling the lives and money of tens of thousands of mesmerized adherents. Or so *McClure's Magazine* and big cities newspapers wrote, without bothering to check facts. The slander against the founder by Mark Twain made people laugh at, and mock, the new denomination. The adverse publicity was so intense that the founder set up, and the church has maintained, a "Committee on Publication" to counteract the negative ideas about the movement and sent out lecturers to set the record straight.

Recent studies by independent researchers, most recently Dr. Gillian Gill at Harvard (Radcliffe Biography Series, 1998) in her new and much-praised, extensive biography *Mary Baker Eddy*, have shown that much of the bad press about Christian Science at the turn of the century involved self-seeking publicity hounds, men angry about women's rights, and disenchanted former friends seeking the spotlight. Just about everybody criticized Mrs. Eddy. She was an easy and interesting target in the days when women's place (especially women who set themselves up as religious leaders) was squarely on the linoleum, in front of the gas range.

And although Mrs. Eddy's reputation as a woman and leader has been significantly redeemed by impartial scrutiny in the last ten years, there is no doubt that the early yellow journalism affected the public perception. Unfavorable comment on the Christian Science Church continued into the twentieth century. Edwin Franden Dakin was one author who wrote a scathing book about the leader and her movement. That biography, too, has been largely discredited by recent researchers such as Gillian Gill for its one-sided, agenda-driven style and factual errors, but impressions gained from reading books like Dakin's remain in the public consciousness.

Eventually, of course, Christian Science was not new any more, and after all, news has to be "new." Criticism continued on into the midpoint of the twentieth century, but ebbed as interest in things religious declined in the 1940s and 50s. Christian Science seemed almost mainline by then. Exposing religious institutions wasn't "in" as political pots boiled publicly and international news coverage dominated the press. Only if you founded a cult which pulled young people from their parents with millennial and dangerous dogma, sometimes to their deaths, could you count on any kind of publicity.

Then, again, criticism of Christian Science began to surface strongly in the 1980s. Today, although Christian Scientists may not often admit it, bad press and public revulsion generated by it, is one of the most important factors in the decline in the church. By then another shift on the part of the public, away from spiritual healing, had also occurred to further complicate the matter.

Criticism reached an apex in the 1980s but it continues to this day. Word in publications like *The Boston Globe*, *Atlantic Monthly* and on a few recent TV programs like "The Practice" has it that Christian Scientists have been left alone too long. They are strange oddballs with dangerous beliefs. They let their children suffer and possibly die in the name of religion. They refuse to go to doctors and live in their communities with unhealed conditions. They lobby legislatures in their state for controversial rights.

Although recent personally driven books, like Caroline Fraser's *God's Perfect Child*, appear to flow from personal wells of bitterness which reflect the apostate's view and are full of distortions, some of the objections raised need to be examined.

Chapter Two

1870—Frightful Medical Practice

Negative press has shaped public views of Mrs. Eddy's religion and the people now practicing it, clearly. And the sad part is that a certain, key part of the recent negative press is true.

Are we as irresponsible as media reports allege? Do we allow unhealed conditions to go on too long, both for ourselves and our children? My own observations about this matter were a long time maturing.

I have been a Christian Scientist for fifty years. Active in the Methodist Church as a teenager and a state Methodist young people's officer, I heard about Christian Science at the very time I was reading the Methodist denominational founder John Wesley's biography, which featured descriptions of Wesley's healing services held on the hills of northern England.

I knew that Jesus had healed the sick, and I was interested in the process. After all, He had said, "Heal the sick, raise the dead, freely you have received, freely give." Shouldn't we think about all of that message if we wished to be devoted followers? Spiritual healing was clearly part of the early work of the church. I did not find the leap to Christian Science from main line Protestantism, or at least Methodism, a large one. More, I recall telling a curious relative, like jumping over a small stream. Methodism had emphasized love and close communion with God and daily Christian discipline, too.

But I had not been totally satisfied there. Wishing to follow

Jesus as carefully as possible, I had questions that could not be answered. I remember being struck by it one night as I sat in a beautiful Gothic sanctuary of North Methodist Church in Indianapolis. "Why do we always say that God may send us good or evil (or allow it)? We always seem to beg him not to do that. Didn't Jesus say, 'Fear not, little flock, for it is your Father's good pleasure to give you the kingdom?' "

When I first began to read some of the articles about Christian Science, I was attracted to the fact that it teaches that God sends us all good, and that it is our job to find out what that good is.

Delving deeper, I found my questions about faith answered; Christian Science was right for me. I married into it and observed that my new husband's grandmother was still going strong after some seventy-seven years in the faith. I stayed with it, and intend to remain right where I am comfortable—in a kind of Christianity which allows me to practice day-by-day total immersion. (Even if I can't always do it.)

Perhaps because I was not born into the religion but chose it, I have an outsider's perspective and can see things which others— those who have been brought up in the faith and sequestered to a certain extent from outside views—cannot see. And what I have seen both keeps me in place because it satisfies me completely when it fulfills the law of Christ for me and works—and has come to trouble me when it doesn't. I don't blame the religion. I take issue with the way Christian Scientists look at themselves—or don't look. We all as a group are allowing bad things to go on and refusing to confront certain problems.

I began to notice as early as the 1970s that there were too many early deaths among our congregations. In the fifty years I've been "C.S." I have seen fifteen to twenty women I knew and cared about in churches where I was involved die in their thirties or forties of ovarian or other female cancers, twenty or thirty men I knew drop dead with untreated heart conditions, both women and men with huge, black skin cancers on their faces refusing treatment, a woman with a large, several-year-old goiter, another woman with a failing liver fading daily before the eyes of all around her for over a year, people dying from pneumonia, the elderly suffering from painful arthritis unable to walk and not finding relief from pain.

These are not crazy folk. Some, most, are devoted Christians for whom their belief has become more important than life itself. These people have made individual choices, choices coming from strength and conviction. My friends outside the church cautiously ask, what is in these people's thinking as they realize that society calls their disease fatal and they may depart this existence? I answer they don't expect to do that, believing ever day healing is coming and with it a deepening of their relationship with God. And if it doesn't—they do not wish to dishonor deep-seated convictions. If sin, disease and death are unreal, they are truly not real and so can never be dignified by admission that a negative condition exists, causing the need to seek medical treatment. It is a logical position in the absolute. But privately I believe that some, many I think, are merely trapped if they just wish to "get well." They are in a social and religious situation that does not allow them to think outside what they believe is the teaching of their church. They believe they can have no alternative but spiritual healing.

As decades passed, however, as I became more and more convinced of the healing power of God as explained in Christian Science, as I became more and more sure that all the force of life resides in God and that we are eternally, perfectly spiritual, I also became convinced that early death among our own frustrates the very purpose of the religion.

People should not suffer and die because of Christian Science. It is not just. The saddest part of all for those who do not find healing in Christian Science and suffer through to the end when there are other options, is that their own church (or perhaps the people within the church, for after all, what is a church but people) has inadvertently betrayed them. More recently, looking into a history of the church through records at the new Mary Baker Eddy Library for the Betterment of Humanity and especially into *Sci-*

ence and Health itself, I became convinced that do-or-die physical healing, hanging on for physical healing, is not what the founder of the religion intended. It is, instead, a function of present church practice evolved over a period of five or more decades and perpetuated after that time. In point of fact, after founding a church based on physical healing—the discovery of a "healing method" which drew in thousands of adherents in the first thirty years of its existence—I think that Mary Baker Eddy ended with a different idea of her new path of religious thinking. It wasn't really just about physical healing. That wasn't even the most important part.

And although careful scrutiny of her own pronouncements and final enunciation of her view of Christianity as shown in the book she wrote, which stands as a study guide interpreting the Bible for over a hundred years, *Science and Health with Key to the Scriptures*, shows that she emphasized something far beyond a physical "healing method," I don't believe all of us as Christian Scientists today honor that emphasis. I hope to remind my denomination that although the religion began in the 1870s as a method of healing sickness through the practice of the all-power of God, by 1900 it had evolved into something much larger—a new and radical view of Christianity which, beginning with total consecration to God as all, would bring the larger results of healing of sin, sickness and death—which Mary Baker Eddy called error. The emphasis had changed in the leader's mind, but ninety years of Christian Science as a movement would prove that, in large part, Christian Scientists wouldn't be able to evolve the way their leader had.

And that inability—a misunderstanding—would affect the lives of the dedicated and sincere people who have suffered and died too young. Like the locomotives of the times sometimes did, we went off the main route and ended up on the siding.

In the early days it did not matter if healing held front and center stage. A religion that promised physical healing was vitally, desperately needed. To understand public perception of Christian Science today, so necessary for us in our desire to survive and grow as branch churches, it is necessary to see what its exact place was in the first three decades of its existence.

What brought people to Mrs. Eddy's revelation then? Christian healing, proven reliable in keeping people healthy and improving conditions in almost miraculous ways for many people, carried the religion along, especially, as has been shown, with the new means of communication. Many did show that the "science" Christian Scientists talked about transformed daily life because of the reliability of the practice of Jesus' laws and the emphasis Mrs. Eddy found on realization of the spiritual identity—and assured adherents of eternal life. But those deeper meanings were not as appealing as the often dramatic testimonies people gave in periodicals and newspapers, later on radio and eventually on TV shows, which concentrated on the healing of bodily conditions. And, admittedly, getting healed of influenza or infertility or asthma certainly wasn't inconsequential. Christian Scientists were showing that the miracles of Jesus were the laws of God for everybody, and that was a profound revelation for the times.

Christian Science got to be known as a method of healing sickness—and that's where it stuck. That's what people wanted anyway—pure and simple—in the days when it was founded. It answered a real need in the days of early death and many fatal illnesses, and the early phase of the religion was designed to meet that need.

It is not especially pleasant to dwell on the "humane brutality" of the medical practice of a hundred years ago, but it is necessary so that we may see in detail what we have all but forgotten. We can only guess how welcome Christian Science was to sufferers of that time. Nineteenth century medical practice was primitive and often ineffective. Well meaning doctors did their best, but it had only been a few years since they were sawing off limbs with dirty saws after giving the patient a dose of chloroform (if they had it) on Civil War battlefields. The conclusions of Lister that both physicians and their instruments ought to be sterile (or at least clean) was just beginning to be accepted when Mrs. Eddy initiated her own healing "practice" in the 1860s. It did not receive wide-spread attention until almost the turn of the last century. So materia medica, which could sometimes help, was just as often terrible and terrifying.

The medical practice of the day involved the whole spectrum of effectiveness, ranging from skilled surgery performed by those trained in Europe or big city colleges in America to quackery and wishful thinking. We have no clear notion today of the despair ill health caused our ancestors of the nineteenth century; it is absolutely dominant in correspondence of the times. Let us look at the year 1884, a few years after that church founding, when in remarkable fashion Christian Science was beginning to catch on, numbering adherents in the thousands and moving through the Midwest into California and Oregon.

Tuberculosis killed 91,000 people in America in 1884—the leading cause of death in the nation that year and other years, according to the annual report of the State Board of Health of the state of Indiana. Pneumonia was usually fatal and killed over 60,000 people in the US in the mid-1880s. Stomach cancer, according to an 1898 internal medicine volume studied by medical students, was considered fatal in virtually every case. The only question was, "How long before he/she dies?"

If you had a baby, it was to be delivered at home, and your chances of dying were drastically increased by "childbed" fever that had plagued women for a thousand years or more. Physicians successfully helped deliver babies, and then mothers chilled, grew feverish and died. Once the fever set in, treatment was not usually effective. It could involve such an odd method as sending carbolic acid into the womb and must have involved great fear and suffering.

A medical society textbook tells of such treatment of a woman after the birth of a child and suffering from high fever:

"Resort was now had to an intra uterine injection of hot water [with carbolic acid] and internal administration of ten grain doses of quinine . . . three distinguished doctors were called in for

consultation . . . more carbolic acid administered." Eight days after the birth, the woman died.

Hiring a wet nurse or giving babies milk from diseased and
ill-fed cows was certain to result in the bad effects of diarrhea,
dehydration and death, so the medical textbooks and popular
health columns in magazines of the times stated. State medical
associations tried to help reverse high childhood mortality rates
by urging mothers to breast-feed their infants themselves.

Most adults were terrified of "going under the knife." To enter a hospital of the day was literally to meet death face-to-face.
My own grandmother died in this period in 1900, from post-oper-
atic shock. A large tumor had been discovered in her uterus at the
birth of her third child, and after the child was delivered, doctors
decided to operate to remove the tumor. She died two days later
of what the newspaper called "a heart attack and shock"—complications of this stressful surgery, in her mid-twenties. She left
three-year-old twins and a newborn.

Although that death was tragic, it was not unusual. Early and
awful death was an expected part of life; the graveyards of the time
are full of tombstones attesting to the power of early death. In
Indiana there were 989 deaths in 1884 of diphtheria and nation-
ally 38,143. Many children did not reach the age of three years,
having been taken away by scourges like scarlet fever, diphtheria
and whooping cough. Vaccinations were gaining in popularity and
beginning to affect the death rate from smallpox, but a significant
part of the population did not have access to them. A micabre but
money-making business in villages in America was the making of
children's caskets with little windows in them so their faces could
be viewed; photographers took after-death photos of women and
men in caskets because so many unexpected deaths left families
without likenesses of their loved ones.

So doctoring was often dangerous, life unpredictable and
Americans were desperate for means to improve health and live
"to a ripe old age"—something the odds didn't favor. People in the
1860s and 70s and 80s could try homeopathic medicine, in which

attenuations of various minerals were given to the patient to stimulate recovery from illness. Mrs. Eddy was an invalid for many years of her young womanhood, and she herself had tried homeopathy and found it interesting, but not effective over the long haul.

Going to see a spiritual healer to improve health was actually not unusual in these days of the infancy of modern medicine. The public did not find it odd to see patients healed through mental means. It was an age of unusual public phenomena, a lot of it connected to mental or physical health. There was mesmerism, whose nineteenth century practitioners demonstrated theatrical hypnotism on stage, and spiritualism, which became a fad in the 1880s and 90s in cities and towns in the United States. Some visitors from beyond would diagnose disease through mediums and ask that the information would be passed along to those sitting around the seance tables. Americans could also go to lectures on phrenology, in which bumps on the head were analyzed to understand personality strengths and difficulties, and even study the new Freudian psychology, which began to trickle into America by the 1890s.

If you could rid yourself of hysteria, you might have a chance to recover physically too, the new theories stated. Newspapers sliding every year deeper into the journalistic sensationalism which has been with us ever since, trumpeted forth the newest odd theories and described the lecture halls full of people seeking The Truth through innovative thought.

A reader in even a small village reading about Christian Science in the papers, could catch up on news of other strange but provocative food for thought along with the morning coffee. One could read advertisements for shipments of shoes just come into the local store, the Franco-Prussian War, General Tom Thumb and the Siamese Twins, Eng and Chang Bunker, the visit of Captain Filbert's dancing dog show van to the field outside town and the latest on a new religion which purported to raise people from their deathbeds, all on the front page.

They read, and many believed—both odd theories and new religion. We have been called the most religious nation in the

West, and this surely comes from our nineteenth century roots. These newspaper readers believed in the power of God, which furthered the easy acceptance of a new religion that emphasized going beyond mere faith in God to understanding of His all-power over every circumstance in life.

Certainly changing your religion, as all these people were doing as they came together in storefronts and homes to form Christian Science churches, was nothing unusual. Neither was having the Christian religion itself change. America had been through several religious revolutions including the coming of Methodism, the founding of the New Light movement on the frontier, the establishment of Shaker communities, and the spread of the doctrine of the Campellitites (the Disciples of Christ). Puritanism had mellowed by the mid-nineteenth century and its descendants, the Presbyterians and Congregationalists, were in the midst of forsaking their harsher doctrines, such as predestination, and were trying to embrace a more liberal form of religion. For real liberals, Unitarianism and Universalism beckoned, promising a non-doctrinal and wide approach to understanding the power of Spirit.

American frontier faith was at its best simple, and that facilitated the acceptance of the Christian Science doctrine that turning over oneself to the all-power of God brought ultimate meaning to existence. Bells chimed from the church "in the valley by the wildwood, no lovelier church in the vale," and inhabitants of Tiffin, Ohio or Hastings, Nebraska, made their way into the small, lovingly decorated sanctuaries. Still, the historic transformation of religious thought from a God of punishment to a God of forgiveness and grace, which had occurred over the entire last century, was by no means complete. With their hearts full of faith in the God of Love, churchgoers still had to often hear about the doctrines of sin and eternal punishment left over from the preaching of the Mathers and Jonathan Edwards in New England. The smell of fire and brimstone hovered over many a heartland church, and was in itself a disincentive to attend.

People recognized the difficulties in that sort of preaching. It was rather frightening, centered on the negative. Those exciting, positive spiritual departures had all occurred in the first half of the nineteenth century. Not much new was happening by the 1880s. In the latter decades of the century, in cities and even in small towns in America, organized religion had petrified to a certain extent, weakened by the skeptical pronouncements of Darwin's disciples and the materialism and economic millennialism that flourishing industrialism spawned.

So whatever Christian Science was, it was destined to make its entrance on an already lit stage, with an audience preconditioned in America to be naturally interested in religion and even mental or spiritual healing, but skeptical (they had just lived through the tales of the tablets of Mormon founder Joseph Smith) and not only avid for gossip but conditioned to sensationalism. It was definitely a hot bed of coals for any religion to walk over.

But beyond the doctrine of an accepting God and man in his own image and likeness that Christian Science was preaching, it must be conceded that the tens of thousands of new converts flocking to the societies and churches forming across the country (probably 400,000 by 1895) were looking for something which would grant them health, cure them of their infirmities and diseases and help them avoid the often atrocious health-care methods of the day. This they could find in the newest thought-method dreamed up by a woman—and attracting new members every day.

For most, it was all about physical healing. The majority of the new members to the cause had heard the central spiritual meat and potatoes message—trust God completely and spititualize thought to cure all ills—and had gone directly to the dessert: feel better fast. Who could blame them? Still, that was a comparatively superficial message which could never hold the train on the tracks, though it took about a century to slow it almost to a halt.

Chapter Three

Off the Track and onto the Siding

Beyond the fact that people were desperate to feel better, and focused largely on the healing aspect of Christian Science in its early days, it has to be asked if there were other factors which allowed the religion to get off the central track of spiritual growth founded on the idea that God is all, matter nothing, and end up on a siding of the railroad I'm suggesting—inordinate emphasis on physical healing.

To understand the factors for what I am calling a wrong turn, we must return to the days before the founding of the church—to an earlier time, when Mary Baker Glover Patterson was too ill and distressed to even take care of her own child and had separated herself from her family.

A key factor in the establishment of Christian Science as a healing method was that the leader herself in that period was concentrating single-mindedly on finding her own much-needed physical healing, and when she found it in such a surprising way, she could think of little else. To read her biography during the 1850s and 1860s, to analyze her own correspondence, is to see day after day of physical suffering. Of course, in worrying about terrible health, as we have shown, she was no different from almost everyone else around her. The population all across the nation was obsessed with health, with secretions and effusions and manipulations which would make them feel better in that age when death seemed always just around the corner.

Mary's search for better health was a long and trying one. In the years before she formed the church in 1879, there were many difficult times and many false starts. Although she was a serious Christian, she had been an invalid for many years and had spent over twenty years trying to be rid of "spinal inflammation," "liver complaint" and other digestive problems. She often seemed to be prostrate on her bed, unable to take care of her own home, suffering from back pain and awful headaches and general weakness.

Christian Scientists know that after she was married to a dentist named Daniel Patterson (following the death of her first husband, George Glover, from yellow fever), and with the child of her first marriage being cared for by others because of her disability, Mary Baker Glover Patterson submitted herself to the inadequate ministrations of physicians and the "water cure" and finally to a paid mental healer known as Phineas Quimby. She was made better for a while in the 1860s after visiting Quimby. A charismatic man in his sixties, Quimby practiced a "talking cure," in which he and the patient focused on the disease. Then he seemed to challenge the disease as a mental aberration and to absorb the ill of the person into himself, even having to wrestle around with what seemed to be devil-like manifestations of the person's ills on his body. Mrs. Patterson was fascinated by the process of mental healing, and in spite of Quimby's disclaimers that he wasn't using religious belief in his work, she believed he was practicing healing as Jesus did. But her ills returned. Much of her mental and physical energy was expended on trying just to feel well enough to get through the day.

But this gifted woman did struggle on. Finding herself increasingly dissatisfied with her irresponsible husband, she lived in near-poverty and tried to write a little poetry and letters-to-the-editor about the passing scene to find relief from her continuing physical complaints. One day in 1866, walking in wintry weather outside her house, she took a serious fall on the ice and was picked up senseless and carried home. She later recounted, and others confirmed, that a physician declared her internal injuries were so serious that she could not live. She called for her Bible and read the healing of the man with palsy in the book of Matthew and rose healed. She was amazed. A period followed in which she read the Bible constantly to try to find out how spiritual healing could operate.

For three years after my discovery, I sought the solution of this problem of Mind-healing, searched the Scriptures and read little else, kept aloof from society and devoted time and energies to discovering a positive rule . . . .I knew the Principle of all harmonious Mind-action to be God, and that cures were produced in primitive Christian healing by holy, uplifting faith; but I must know the Science of this healing, and I won my way to absolute conclusions through divine revelation, reason and demonstration. (p. 109 S&H)

She came to the conclusion, through revelation as she insisted, that the prayerful acknowledgment of God's all-power and the subsequent conviction of the unreality of material sense or conditions would bring about physical healing. Wanting to share the benefits of what she had found (and also hoping for some sort of small income), she began a "healing practice." Many times the patients seemed to improve or be healed in a way some of them felt was miraculous. She concentrated on healing; it was perfectly natural. Hers was a great and Divinely-inspired discovery to improve the health of mankind. It was accepted by many thousands as such, and the times made it relatively easy to sell.

When Mary herself began to practice healing based on the methods of Jesus, when she began to accept patients and visit bedsides to heal cases of chronic and non-chronic illness, she became allied with a tradition common in the frontier period, that of the "preacher-doctor." Railed against by medical and ministerial associations, these dual practitioners would pray and treat in the same visit. They asked for Divine help in casting out sickness. Most Americans believed health was the natural state of man, that God made man free. But the Fall of Man complicated everything and the preachers were there to help with all that. They could pray for you, and then cut off a carbuncle from your leg, right on the kitchen table. Prayers of thanksgiving for successful treatment would follow. That process could relieve pain and inflammation and might make you a better person as well. It accounted for the success of these preacher-doctors, who advertised in newspapers in many towns. It was important for people in the late nineteenth century to be good Christian people. Non-invasive healing based on Christ's healing was a very appealing idea to many.

Still poor as a churchmouse and having difficulty supporting herself, as early as 1867 Mary had taken her first student, a shoemaker named Hiram Crafts, and instructed him in the principles of spiritual healing that she had herself found: declare with the patient in prayer, much as Jesus did, that God has all power and evil or disease have no real hold on you and your faith and conviction will be realized in a healthy body. Mary lived with Crafts and his wife for a while, one of the many temporary homes in which she sheltered during this difficult period in her life. Hiram set up shop and advertised in the local paper that he could cure "consumption, catarrh, scrofula, dyspepsia and rheumatism." He took patients but, unfortunately, could not afford to live on what the few patients paid him. Others came to learn to heal from Mary and also took patients, just as doctors did. I am reiterating much of what Christian Scientists know well, but it is important to establish the predominance of physical healing in the earliest period.

There was a need to commit to paper what was happening successfully in this prayerful practice. And so eight years before she would found a church, Mary began to write a Bible commentary which would describe what she was developing as a practitioner of "primitive Christianity." It included the healing of disease through enlightened prayer and chapters on related subjects like "Creation" and "Natural Science." She was beginning to call her own discovery and teaching a "science." Her first truly serious and successful student, Richard Kennedy, began to practice this healing science in 1870. Charming and pleasant, Kennedy soon had lines of would-be patients at his door, near Mary's residence in Lynn, Massachusetts. So many people claimed themselves healed of various complaints that she soon offered classes in "metaphysical" healing.

Most Christian Scientists know how trying this period was to the leader. Soon some of the students began to fall away, sometimes from the healing method itself; more often from the direction of the strong-minded leader and author. A serious schism developed between Kennedy and his tutor in spiritual healing and they tormented each other in the press and through other means for years to come. Thus began a process which eventually gave Mary Baker Eddy almost constant trouble: the personality of the healers who learned at this woman's side and then conspicuously fell away. These people became known by public and press for unbridled success in "healing practice" but also for rebellion and noisy attacks on their former leader. By 1870 this process was in full swing.

The point is that in the early 1870s there was little real understanding that this woman was founding a church. What she was espousing, everyone believed, was a Godly healing method. That was the news. Jesus wanted us to heal; this was His method, the method of healers like Peter and Paul in the early church. She surely began to cherish ideas in the ten years before the founding of the church that all of this would develop into some sort of more formal movement. She told Kennedy that "Some day church bells will chime my birthday."

In this earliest "testing time," Mrs. Patterson was trying to define, and refine, her own method. Her Bible commentary was coming along, as in her personal life her divorce from her dentist husband Daniel Patterson became final. She continued to move from lodging to lodging, trying to find a way to support herself with no income and little family help. Her relatives found embarrassing her publicly proclaimed "science," and classes in which she turned out healers. Her strong personality and claims to religious enlightenment—"revelation"—generated jealousy, suspicion and mockery.

All along this road, however, it was the belief of her followers and the public that this was all about getting well from sickness. What a blessing it was for their age!

In 1875 she published that first edition of *Science and Health*, the landmark book which described her ideas of healing practice based on Jesus's work. She stated her theology: all the problems of the mortal scene are caused by the belief that man is separated from God. Indeed, that separation is not so, she affirms. Life is about unwinding the beliefs of the material world and standing clearly and spiritually as the child of God's creating, perfect and immortal. "There must be a going out of personal sense and coming in of the spiritual, to understand the science of being and to give a higher sense of Omnipotence whereby to control man and matter," she wrote.

Clearly, this was about a larger truth than just getting well from symptoms of headache and flu. The spiritual center of Christian Science is all right there in the book. It seems clear, however, that Mary herself did not understand the full implications of the view of being that she was espousing. She later admitted that during the sixties and seventies ideas were only starting to develop, as she tried to listen only to God. She was attempting to articulate what Divine Revelation was giving her, and succeeding only partially. Time would take care of that.

Not only was she, and everybody around her, focused on physical healing, but the woman herself was troubled by the many facets of spreading the gospel, preaching in the meeting halls where it was being espoused, teaching both healers and teachers to spread the word, and living the life of a newly hatched religious leader pretty much under fire the whole time. It was hard to pay attention to long-term directions.

Still, *Science and Health* is a landmark book in the history of religious writing in the nineteenth century. In this first edition of *Science and Health*, Mary's syntax is convoluted, her ideas jump around like rabbits in some places, and critics have tirelessly pointed out errors in spelling and grammar, but the meaning is there: turn to God and live your life as a spiritual child of God. Deny the ultimate validity of material life, which is unreal and has no claim on you and depend on Spirit. Then you will find meaning, health and fulfillment. Chapters on "Creation," "Prayer and Atonement" and "Physiology" as well as the others already mentioned, all take the reader through a spiritual journey away from material living and into absolute truth. Gillian Gill has noted that Mrs. Eddy's arguments about the nothingness of evil and the allness of God are reminiscent of St. Augustine's musings on the very subject.

But if Mary was going metaphysical with the publication of this book and calling for life-changing shifts in perspective towards God, her students were rushing about setting up healing practices, putting out shingles on their front walks, like doctors and lawyers. Still, by 1879 when that group of students met to form with their leader the Christian Science Church, the scene described in the first chapter, that action pointed the way to larger goals. The earlier and informal group of students, which had called itself the Christian Science Association, soon became The Church of Christ, Scientist, a church designed to "commemorate the word and works of our Master, which should reinstate primitive Christianity and its lost element of healing." That was a large vision. The horizon was expanding rapidly beyond the healing of the sick, though nobody could see that quite clearly at the time.

Each year brought progress. In 1877 Mary had married one of her new students, Asa Gilbert Eddy, thus taking the name by which she would be known to posterity. He was a serene, courteous man whose aplomb served his leader (and wife) well through the contentious years she was entering.

Students fell away, relatives deserted; court cases were filed as the 70s became the 80s. Mrs. Eddy herself felt malicious mental forces were being directed at her from former adherents of the new healing method. She fought, and was fought against in the courts for money owed her, and for odd plots against her former students in which she herself was supposed to be implicated. But the small group of faithful followers who met in Lynn and then in Boston to share prayer and listen to Mrs. Eddy talk earnestly about the necessity for trusting God, the ground of ultimate reality, in every aspect in life and denying the impositions of material life as unreal, grew weekly through the late 70s and early 80s. And as she began to broaden her ministry, to speak in churches around New England and beyond, it grew even faster. More and more people were healed and publications in wider numbers began to document these healings.

As the 80s unfolded, the students who learned from Mrs. Eddy and went out to heal multiplied exponentially, setting up hundreds of healing practices in other parts of Massachusetts, Chicago, Milwaukee, and even in Europe. Early adherents were the students of Mrs. Eddy at her informal teaching sessions and soon at the Massachusetts Metaphysical College she set up; others just read the book and wrote to Mrs. Eddy and put up the sign in the window. As people began to read *Science and Health* (some with perplexity at its rather poured-out and jammed up syntax, many with inspiration, sensing something revolutionary) hundreds of other men and women who had never met Mary Baker Eddy put notes in local papers and "took up the practice."

Not untypical was a Methodist minister in New York State named Severin Simonsen, who later wrote that he spoke to his congregation one Sunday and told them he was leaving the ministry of their church to take up the ministry of healing. The next day he put his notice as a Christian healer in the newspaper. Since he had a wife and small children, he had to overcome trepidation that there would not be a living wage in the practice of Christian Science. He wrote that he had to trust God no matter what. There could be no worrying about piling up bills, no figuring in ledgers, no getting up late at night to pore over the figures. He needed to put the bills in the drawer, deny their power, and ignore these signs of trouble. What was needed was focus on healing. Patients did come and he found success.

Of course, *Science and Health* improved; edition after edition came out during this period as Mrs. Eddy's understanding deepened.

The spread of Christian Science through town and country-side was attested to by a remarkable deluge of healings reported in local and national periodicals. What exactly was the nature of these healings, putting the stamp of physical cure indelibly on the religion? A perusal of the chapter called "Fruitage" in the last edition of *Science and Health*, at least, makes us guess that quite honestly a portion of them were healings of "hysteria," a common Victorian complaint. It was usually attributed to women and was blamed on their reproductive systems; probably it was a condition caused by unhappiness and lack of direction and productivity in a male-dominated society. Its symptoms were nervousness, stomach trouble, biliousness, weariness and depression, ailments often cited in the testimonies.

Another portion seems to have been caused by general unhappiness and bad mental attitude. Some primary care physicians today report that in any given year from 40 percent to as high as 80 percent of cases they see have attitudinal, rather than primarily physical, problems. Coming upon an intensely positive life direction Christian Science offered would have turned many lives and attitudes around, thus resulting in healing. The connection of mind and body is a given today in medical science. No one knows the extent of the immense influence on the immune system and general mechanism for health in the body that a calm and peaceful mind, centered if you will, can bring. The attitudinal change that Christian Science can bring to an entire life should not be underestimated.

But many, many of these early healings were authentic cures of chronic disease. Men, women and their children who had been diagnosed by physicians as having rheumatism (arthritis), heart disease, asthma, cancer, tuberculosis and colitis found themselves cured.

Today a renewed interest in spiritual healing is permeating traditional denominations, and Presbyterians, Episcopalians, Catholics and others are holding healing services, following the injunctions of the Book of James—"And the prayer of faith shall save the sick,"—appointing healing ministries and experiencing their own sickbed cures. Probably Christian Science's thousands of declared and often physician-authenticated healings for over one-hundred twenty years have contributed to the growing interest in the prayer that can heal.

To many who have witnessed or heard about these cures they seem miraculous, but Mrs. Eddy and the early followers believed they were the law of God in operation: God intends for each of us to dwell in His perfect love and that includes our physical as well as spiritual health. Understand this in deep, prayerful communion with God and you will be healed.

When I first became a Christian Scientist in Indianapolis there were those who testified to being quickly cured in the influenza outbreak after World War I, others had been cured of late-stage tuberculosis, and those given up to pneumonia who rose from bed, made well.

A man in our own church had been given up for dead from lockjaw in the days before tetanus inoculation became common. His sisters often spoke of knowing their brother was in agony upstairs with his jaws locked, out of his head. They spent three days in prayer and he was well by the end of those three days. To read *The Christian Science Sentinel* and the *Journal* from the period 1885-1944 is to see testimony after testimony to the power of prayer to heal the sick.

Can my friends who doubt and those in the media who scorn today believe these thousands of people? Is it self-deception or misdiagnosis, or the exaggeration of the credulous? Does something also actually happen at Lourdes? What it is? What about the young girl I knew in northern Michigan who had the very rare form of female hemophilia, walking with braces on her legs and missing school weeks at a time. Is she rambling into invention when she tells of feeling power course through her body at a charismatic Catholic healing service, and walking free ever after, even twenty years later. How can the doctor who treated her for years declare she is free from hemophilia? Is he lying? I saw the effects of that transformation myself. Was I hallucinating?

Likewise, what are all those testimonies to healing in Christian Science about? I ask my Christian friends from other traditions if these healings may not point to a little understood basic principle of nature and life itself. Harvard is sponsoring a long-range study on the power of the spirit to heal, involving many disciplines in both the religious and the medical community. We do not know how bodies respond to the power of prayer, but we know they do. People report feelings of warmth rushing through their bodies, the presence of positive force or overwhelming love, which eliminates pain and suffering. My daughter-in-law, not a Christian Scientist, reports that the physician she took our granddaughter to see at Dartmouth Medical Center for a serious inner ear infection told her he employs the power of prayer consciously to assist the healing. Scores of doctors adopt this position because they believe prayer helps and heals. Christian Scientists have known this for years.

In the early history of the Christian Science church countless spectacular healings were the "signs and wonders" which accompanied the founding of the religious denomination. By 1889 Londoners were flocking to the lectures on Christian Science, standing room only, to witness the phenomenon. Almost every large city in America had a thriving community of Christian Scientists by then. Mrs. Eddy's discovery had become a religious phenomenon unequalled in American history, garnering over a half million adherents by the turn of the century.

The Mother Church, the First Church of Christ, Scientist, Boston, Massachusetts, began to rise in 1894 in a reclaimed area of Boston, and the new church societies began to raise their own edifices in small and large towns, hiring prominent architects, paying them through donations from the grateful healed.

So church building became a focus as well as spiritual healing. At first there were "preachers" and choirs; soon Mrs. Eddy, feeling the necessity of devoting herself to church growth, resigned as Pastor of the Mother Church, stipulating that her growing church would use the Bible and *Science and Health* as its only preachers, with lesson sermons on a selected series of topics to be read by elected readers instead of ordained clergy. In Traverse City, Michigan, a group of eager adherents in the 1890s rented space above a grocery store and, when they got the word from Boston, switched from a choir to a soloist. There were to be few social events at the churches, reserving the buildings for sacred service. Never mind, it was the healing power that drew people in.

By the mid 1890s with the church she had never planned mature, Mrs. Eddy seems to have moved in a direction she had grasped almost from the beginning of her work and which took her away from the "sensational healing" interpretation of what she was doing. She began in the 1890s to emphasize the founding of a new form of Christianity instead of just a method of healing.

A study of the evolution of the several versions of *Science and Health* demonstrates that direction. The later editions are quite different from the first. Mockers and critics contend a rather dippy old lady was finally getting her grammar and syntax straight, but a careful reading shows the progressive deepening of the theology and purpose of Christian Science in the book. It was moving far beyond the puffery in newspaper ads which advised, "Discover how you can use Christian Science to get rid of rheumatism, catarrh, and prolapsed female organs."

I think one can show there are several reasons for the gradual evolution in Mrs. Eddy's thought. In the first place, Mrs. Eddy had truly come to believe that the science she had discovered was much larger than just physical healing. Why? No doubt most of the reasons for her enlarging the scope of Christian Science from that first edition and those first few healers hanging shingles out had to do with her own secure position as a Christian leader by 1890. She had been tentative in the early days, trying to fathom the meaning of her own spiritual revelation, to sense the direction it would take. Thirty years had passed; she had found out who she was and what tiger she had by the tail. She never ceased to turn to God for direction, and what He revealed and ordered sent her deeper and deeper.

Another major reason for looking for an ever more profound slant on the Christianity she loved and which she would contribute to the Christian world was that there were practical problems with the "all-out healing" focus the movement had early taken and was still deeply involved with twenty-five years later. With thousands of healers around the country and now the world in the 1890s, things were sometimes going awry. The personalities of the healers, practitioners as they were called, came to predominate over the central spiritual core of the religion: Trust God as the all-power of the Universe and life will work for you. Instead, in some cases, it became "trust me (and pay the fee) and I'll see you through."

In small towns, those who needed help (the dependent and unhappy as well as the sick) gravitated to the offices of the practitioner. I explain to my friends that practitioners are those who devote themselves to the public practice of praying for those in need using prayers of affirmation, trust and surrender. They charge modestly, or if the sufferer cannot pay, not at all for their help. Christian Science practitioners do not use medicine in their treatment. They are not today usually dramatic figures, as they were in the early days, but instead people of quiet confidence born of years of experience in the faith.

But then early practitioners, often Christian Scientists for a year or less, had, or assumed, the power of charismatic spiritual leaders in Bicknell, Indiana or Cheboygan, Wisconsin. They became gurus, counselors in matters of marriage (Mrs. Eddy, an odd candidate for marriage counselor, had a chapter in *Science and Health* on the subject), arguments between relations in the small towns, conflicts with their mothers-in-law and the challenges of raising of children as well as physical problems. The problem of personalization on the part of practitioners and teachers of Christian Science in local communities has continued to this day; if a practitioner or teacher of Christian Science says "do it," it gets done. These are People of Spiritual Authority. And, of course, many times they are good counselors and high achievers in the demonstration of the faith. But sometimes not.

Mrs. Eddy was well aware that "personal sense" was out there in the boondocks, stalking the new religion and gaining power for a few dynamic healers who seemed to forget their leader back home in Boston and the purpose of what they were doing. People grateful for healing showered gifts on the healers, spent hours with them and got emotionally involved on a human level. And then they got disgruntled. The letters of the early church show some converts taking Mrs. Eddy's classes, going out to heal, and going back into the Baptist Church denouncing her six months later when they couldn't make a living or their healing work failed, replete with sour attitudes toward the new phenomenon.

Sometimes the healers were getting it wrong—terribly wrong. Mrs. Eddy had had to Part Company, bitterly, with that first student/healer Richard Kennedy, partly because he had "rubbed" people's heads (an outlawed practice) as he prayed with them. Many of the enthusiastic women who were sent forth by Mrs. Eddy to establish Christian Science communities, and head them up as pastors in these early days, were carried away on waves of self adulation and ecclesiastical power.

We can be reminded that in the late 1880s and in the 90s, Mrs. Eddy had to deal with Augusta Stetson, a charismatic practitioner who had founded First Church of Christ, Scientist in New York City. She was an effective healer, and she recruited twenty-five healers to join her in an elegant complex of healing offices. There they conducted services for the fashionable and powerful scions of New York society who became followers of the Stetson version of Christian Science.

Augusta taught a personalized, effusive version of Christian Science, believing that Mrs. Eddy was somehow Divine and would continue to guide her after the founder's passing from the earth. *The New York Herald* had a field day describing weird happenings in the New York church. Augusta Stetson expected to succeed Mrs.

Eddy as head of the entire church and she had to be rebuked and finally disavowed. In the meantime many people had distorted ideas about what Christian Science was through learning about it from the big-city branch.

All kinds of derivative ideas about the healing method surfaced. Some practitioners began "visualizing"—if the liver was diseased, picture a healthy liver. (Some cancer therapy today emphasizes positive visualization, but it was not a part of Mrs. Eddy's teaching.) Others were personally flamboyant, with notorious habits which titillated readers of newspapers in both the United States and Canada. Mrs. Josephine Woodbury set up a popular practice in Canada, encouraging her followers to practice mystical or magic aberrations of Christian Science or adopt monasticism to produce healing. She was eventually accused of flagrant immorality, producing a son with someone who was not her husband and ridiculously calling her pregnancy an immaculate conception and naming her son "Prince" after the Prince of Peace. No wonder people guffawed to read of these doings in the papers.

So there was a superficiality, and often corrupted practice in the "healing method" approach that must have disgusted and bewildered Mrs. Eddy, who wished people to see the revelation as a new form of Christianity, uniting all denominations, reforming lives. The written record in the Mary Baker Eddy Library in Boston supports these contentions.

Little by little the reformation of lives, the essential message of the Gospel, came to predominate in Mrs. Eddy's thought. It had been there all along, but overshadowed by the dramatics of bodily healing.

It was the concept of salvation in a new and dynamic form: Commit totally to Christ, know your full salvation as a perfect and eternal child of God, who is Love, and all right things are possible to you. Physical Healing will follow, as well as all else. By the final edition of *Science and Health* the emphasis is almost totally on Living the Way, overcoming sin as well as sickness and death through the realization of God's all power. It is a broadened and enlarged tent for certain, emphasizing total transformation of the human experience to conform to the ideal of the perfect Christ. Though she called for "healers, more healers," through the last couple of decades of her life, realizing that healing of all sorts was at the core of her revelation, she had enlarged her perspective of that healing to include all of Mankind for the universal blessings of Divine Love. The founding of *The Christian Science Monitor* is an example of the outreach that goes beyond physical healing: she came to see healing as the curing of the world of its false dependencies on powers other than God.

One infinite God, good, unifies men and nations; constitutes the brotherhood of man; ends wars; fulfils the Scripture, "Love thy neighbor as thyself;" annihilates pagan and Christian idolatry—whatever is wrong in social, civil, criminal, political and religious codes; equalizes the sexes, annuls the curse on man, and leaves nothing that can sin, suffer, be punished or destroyed. (p.340 S&H)

Also significant in her expansion of the purpose of Christian Science was the fact that all-out emphasis on healing had damaging consequences when it failed. And fail it did, of course, at times. Notorious cases of practitioners who took on seemingly hopeless cases of patients against the wishes of their families, secreted them away from "animal magnetism" on the parts of their families and then couldn't help them were exposed in the newspapers.

In our own family a young niece of my husband's grandfather was accepted as a patient about 1920 by a Christian Science practitioner. Her problem was a congenital heart problem. She seemed blue and unable to lead an active life. "You are free," the practitioner assured her. "You don't need to feel restriction." According to family tradition, this niece was taken to a resort where she stayed with a practitioner, the family no doubt agreeing to anything that might help their daughter, who couldn't be helped by the physicians of the time. Newly "freed," the young woman played an active game of tennis and then died soon afterward.

From the turn of the century on and certainly before, the newspapers which were reporting the miraculous healing of scores of victims of disease were also reporting the failure of Christian Science at times as a healing method.

In a famous court case much carried by the media, a practitioner refused treatment for her own daughter at childbirth and both the mother and child died. Criminal charges were brought against the practitioner. The ever continuing bad press became more of a problem than ever, as well as more lawsuits by grieving victims. Too many promises had been made; sometimes they didn't work out.

Did Mrs. Eddy intend her followers to pursue physical healing through her methods forever, even when it was not bringing results? To die for it? It is my strong belief that by 1890 she came to be aware of the trap her church members could fall into, to say nothing of the lawsuits, so by the turn of the century, and as she finalized the revelation, she allowed for escapes in the case spiritual healing did not bring results.

The case for her conviction that do-or-die healing in her church was not productive can be made in a strong manner by reading her own words:

• *If Christian Scientists ever fail to receive aid from other Scientists—their brethren upon whom they may call—God will still guide them into the right use of temporary and eternal means. Step by step will those who trust Him find that—"God is a refuge and strength, a very present help in trouble." (p. 444 S&H)*

• *Healing physical sickness is the smallest part of Christian Science. It is only the bugle-call to thought and action, in the higher range of infinite goodness. The emphatic purpose of Christian Science is the healing of sin. (Rudimental Divine Science)*

• *If, from an injury or from any cause, a Christian Scientist were seized so with pain so violent that he could not treat himself mentally—and the Scientists had failed to relieve him—the sufferer could call a surgeon who would give him a hypodermic injection, then when the belief of pain was lulled, he could handle his own case mentally. (p. 464 S&H)* [Although she was generally healthy and strong after her years of conversion, at the end of her life she suffered from agonizing pain from a kidney stone and called for morphine more than once, thus in her own way legitimizing medication for the relief of serious pain, a part of history some Christian Scientists have chosen to ignore.]

• [In a letter February 19, 1900, to her grown son George Glover, then living in the Dakotas, who, attempting to follow his mother's teachings, believed his children should not be vaccinated] *But if it was my child I should let them vacinate [sic] him and then with Christian Science would prevent its harming the health of my child.*

• [To Dr. Alfred E. Baker, her cousin who was an MD, an obstetrician who had taken up Christian Science and wished to know if assisted deliveries were still possible for those he was teaching "scientific obstetrics"]: *If [you] cannot demonstrate delivery, you may resort to instruments. Suffer it to be so now.* Bound volumes at the Mary Baker Eddy library correspondence for December 20, 1898.

• [To a relative asking about another cousin, Mrs. Lechman, who was struggling with an unhealed physical ailment] *Tell her to retain the MD. It will be a defense in this hour and it cannot harm her.*

These definite statements about the need to qualify dedicated effort towards healing with humanity and common sense seem to have been brushed aside by both the movement and the public at the time. So physical healing, no matter what, became the central focus of interest in Christian Science in America—in spite of its founder's clearly stated views that there are good reasons for looking for alternate means of healing when Christian Science fails to heal.

Nobody was listening, probably because of the intense focus on the founder's personality at 1900. Critical articles centering on the founder became even more vituperative with the turn of the century. A notorious series by Georgine Milmine edited by Willa Cather and others in *McClure's Magazine* scornfully heaped allegations of vanity, greed, duplicity, and general strangeness of personality on Mrs. Eddy. Mark Twain piled on with the satirical and slanted sendup mentioned earlier, which made some of Christian Science's beliefs seem ridiculous.

But it was not only the stern lessons of the school of hard knocks that effected a change in Mrs. Eddy, which led her away from single-minded emphasis on bodily healing as the all-in-all. Mrs. Eddy was, herself, maturing as a Christian. Beset by all kinds of problems in a church grown successful and wealthy by 1900, surrounded by controversies and those who resented her and were causing trouble within and without the movement, fawned over by adoring adherents who wished to worship her, she tried increasingly to shut herself off with a few loyal students and work for the maturation and expansion of a denomination which now numbered close to half a million people. And she turned increasingly to the Christ and found her only comfort—and answers—for the future of the church she had founded.

Look at the far horizon, Mrs. Eddy seemed to be saying. Christian Science was a wide, new explanation of Christianity, and mankind must understand it in this way or it would never understand it at all. It was about healing in the broadest sense, not solely about quick fix (or even long-term) physical healing. ". . . and the leaves of the tree were for the healing of the nations," the Bible says.

The final edition of *Science and Health* (1910 but almost the same as her 1902 edition) is radically different from the first edition. Given that several hands had had a part in the grammatical and organizational differences, given that there had been experiments that failed along the way, replaced by others—the final edition of *Science and Health* is a dynamic and brilliant textbook for leading the Christian life, as well as a full exposition of Christian Science. It is not about hanging out shingles to cure stomach aches.

The comparison of first and last edition is extraordinary if one wants to understand the place bodily healing should have in this religion.

The first edition attempted to explain the new method of

healing, setting it in its place in a theology which insisted on the unreality of evil and sickness. It is a limited canvas on which Mrs. Eddy's newly emerging ideas about the nothingness of matter are painted in dim and shadowy shapes. It does not attempt to deal in any grand way with the changes necessary for "the Christianization of daily life" and the universal salvation of mankind (based in this case on a full recognition of selfhood as spiritual, belonging solely to God).

In the final edition of *Science and Health* the destruction of sin (and death to a more limited extent) becomes an equal, or even more important goal than the destruction of sickness. Sin was mentioned only ninety some times in the entire first edition. The threat or destruction of sin is alluded to one hundred fifteen times in the first three chapters of the final edition alone, over a thousand times in the full text of the book. But more important than the mention of the word sin (often with sickness and death as a trilogy) to be confronted and destroyed with the omnipotent power of God, are the specifics about how to fight the good fight over sin.

And what is Mrs. Eddy's conception of sin, a condition hardly mentioned today by Christian Scientists, along with almost every other Christian belief system, but absolutely paramount in the teachings of Jesus and his chief disciples and followers including Mrs. Eddy? Sin was to Mary Baker Eddy any obstacle which seems to separate man from the God who loves him totally. Thus its eradication becomes a necessity to man's spiritual improvement. You can't be well or whole in any sense of the words if you act as if you are separated from your Creator. So healing follows the eradication of sin in consciousness, the only place it can exist. Beyond this separation concept, however, was this daughter of Congregational New England's conviction that the Bible tells us exactly what sin is, through the Ten Commandments and Jesus' and Paul's admonitions. Wrong acting, adultery, greed, envy, maliciousness and all the rest, might be a false belief, but as long as we were immersed in it we could not progress—and we caused pain to others. It needed to be stopped—before healing could even commence usually.

Every page in the last edition is loaded with specific advice on how to do that, on transcending to the spiritual life, on the Christian walk. (This is also true in Mrs. Eddy's other prose works, most created after the first edition of *Science and Health* and not included in the discussion here.) We can share her timeless view, a vista far beyond the tired pleasures and pains of daily life. "We should forget our bodies in remembering good and the human race." "We worship spiritually, only as we cease to worship materially." "Reflecting God's government, man is self-governed." It is the one most inspired, and at the same time most practical, self-help book beyond the Bible on practicing Christianity that has ever been written.

We should make no mistake: healing the sick is just as strong a commandment in the final edition as the first, and the book's insistence on Christian healing puts healing sickness in the forefront. In fact, the seal on the front of the book is the central and foremost command: "Heal the sick, raise the dead, cast out demons, cleanse the lepers." But in the final edition of *Science and Health* the Christian part of Christian Science has come to the forefront, reflecting the founder's increasing absorption with, and love of, the Christ.

Interestingly, Jesus was a shadowy and relatively unimportant figure in the first edition; now He is front and center as the revolutionary and Divine figure who brought a new method of living and salvation to mankind, a rather more traditional view than she had been espousing before this time. Christian Science proposes to extend the Master's teaching in a special way in a new age: it centers on the specifics of practicing Jesus's teachings—"primitive Christianity"—by describing them in terms of nineteenth century science. Jesus told of the life that brings salvation to His world. He made the natural law of God seem good for all mankind.

Jesus' pronouncements and promises could really be viewed as the laws of the Universe. "Ye shall know the truth and the truth shall make you free." "He that liveth and believeth on me shall have everlasting life." These truths, laws, practiced rigorously and with complete belief in God's all power, could lead to the true benedictions of Christian living. It was not exactly new: the *Imitation of Christ* by Thomas à Kempis made the same arguments; Mrs. Eddy clad her ideas in the garments of 19th century science. And none of these things are possible without the removal of the impediment of sinful belief and thinking, which can be done with God's good grace. "And God leadeth us not into temptation but delivereth us from sin, sickness and death," Mrs. Eddy says in her spiritual interpretation of the Lord's Prayer.

Fundamentalists both in her own day and today have complained that the view of Jesus and his mission to destroy sin and sickness departs from traditional Christian theology: that Christian Scientists do not properly afford Him the status of divinity, that they do not accept the Trilogy, do not believe in being "born again" or in the sacrament of baptism, or hell as a place. A few of these things are true at some level. But scriptural interpretation in many denominations has evolved so that many of these doctrines are being interpreted in broader ways, some similar to those of Mrs. Eddy. Recent books by mainline (not Evangelical) Protestant thinkers, for example, espouse views on the Atonement which move away from the "blood of the lamb" into a broader view. This is that Jesus' sacrifice is seen as effecting at-one-ment with God, exactly Mrs. Eddy's position. Both views can be justified from the broad tones of the Biblical narrative.

Mrs. Eddy had moved from healing method to Larger Truth. The final edition of *Science and Health* is saturated not only with Jesus the Christ but with the Bible, which Mrs. Eddy had come to study and increasingly love daily through the thirty years which had passed from first to last edition. *Science and Health* cannot be understood without its companion piece, the Bible, and indeed Mrs. Eddy subtitled later editions: *Science and Health with Key to the Scriptures*. That's how she intended for her book to be used, as a companion piece to the Bible.

The last edition of her textbook is a confident espousal of the triumph of the spiritual over the physical, for healing the physical, mental and spiritual ills of the world and establishing the Kingdom of God as a present reality. It is soundly positive, filled with faith and reverence and good advice on living "on the mountain," so serene with the assurance of trials overcome and lives improved over three decades that it fairly trumpets forth unquenchable faith in God. I think *Science and Health* is, in its final edition, a chariot of fire. Having passed through its own furnace experiences based on the suffering of its author and the message it conveyed, it guards and guides with Divine assurance to those who will open their eyes to see.

It would take another generation to take the gift it had been given—the book and the movement which grew out of it—and make what it would of it. Two traditions had emerged from the founding period of Christian Science: a method to heal bodily sickness, and a freshly new interpretation of Christianity. These two traditions would contend during the century to come, and when the one won out, it would come to threaten the very existence of the movement. The times to come would not be for the fainthearted in the age after the leader had gone.

Chapter Four

The Chariot of Fire Cools Down

If, as I contend, Mrs. Eddy had become well aware of the dangers even in her time of do-or-die healing, of lawsuits and terrible press and the danger of appearing to be odd and unreasonable; if she put escape clauses into her directions to the church, telling them they had the freedom to make choices about healing if they failed to find relief; if she herself sought morphine injections in her very last years when tormented by pain and never condemned anybody for doing that; and finally, if she herself had come to see her science in broadly inclusive terms of salvation—and if all these things are true, how then did Christian Scientists fall into the "never go to doctors even if you're dying" mindset, which I contend has brought bad PR and helped send the movement into decline?

One main reason is that it's admirable and logical to go the full way. The very process of seeking healing spiritually encourages persistence. If you're trying to pray your way through a problem, when do you stop? Those who want to trust God want to keep at it until what they need happens—all religions teach that. If you give up, your prayed-for goal may be just around the corner. Remember the old adage of the rock and sledgehammer.

Another is that if one temporizes, gives up on Christian healing when it gets life-threatening or very hard, it may tend to dilute or weaken the strength of the healing power when one wishes to utilize it in the future.

With Christian Scientists, "giving up" has even more dire

implications. We may be seen to be failed Christians if we give up and consult a doctor when we are in sincere physical distress.

Interestingly, one of the very strengths of the spiritual map for Christian Scientists, the last edition of *Science and Health*, inadvertently contributed to the decline of the movement as a denomination in the twentieth century. Mrs. Eddy's clear direction for the individual Christian who would find healing is that he take up the cross and follow Jesus in the everyday life, demonstrating God's total control as Jesus did. Spiritual growth, demonstrated on a daily basis, would result in healing.

Christian Scientists came to be dedicated not only to that injunction, but also to an inversion of it that Mrs. Eddy never intended: If it's true that you demonstrate your increased spirituality by healing (and this all-too-often came to mean physical healing) then it is also true, they reasoned, that if you aren't demonstrating physical healing you aren't growing spiritually. In short, you are letting not only yourself but God down if you don't stick with it until you find physical healing. No matter what, through pain and suffering, all will contribute to your spiritual growth and that is what all Christians are after. Persistence in faith is the exemplary side. There is another, of course, which may have elements of narrow-mindedness involved. Or, as a friend of mine said about those who commit to do-or-die healing, "They think you won't get into heaven if you give up and give in."

When I was expecting a baby at seven months, and premature labor began, and I finally decided on an emergency Caesarian section in a hospital when complications continued, someone in the Christian Science institution where I taught said, "I knew her demonstration wasn't up to the level it should be. Her spiritual understanding fell short." In other words, I'd failed myself and my baby. What a devastating burden to have to carry, along with a child's death.

Today that inversion, bringing with it the implication that a person "hasn't demonstrated healing as yet and needs more spiritual growth" continues to cause major problems for those in Christian Science church communities. There is a determination to "hold on" and "hang in there" in spite of major unhealed conditions, thus causing concern (and sometimes anger) on the part of family members and bypassing the ability to have the condition diagnosed in a reasonable amount of time, let alone to consider alternatives for getting well after a period of time. Let us admit the premise that this do-or-die attitude towards healing among Christian Scientists reflects sincere desire for growth in knowing and reflecting God's government in personal life. The people who maintain it would at times rather choose dying with a problem than abandoning their commitment to God, as they see it. If error is unreal, it is unreal, period and we discard our very view of reality by abandoning the quest for healing through Spirit.

Christian Science practitioners are particularly on trial when dire physical problems occur. They have devoted their lives to healing and are thoroughly committed to the spiritual way of physical help. Can they then just go get chemotherapy or surgery when large lumps appear on their bodies? Ask for diagnosis—possibly treatment for macular degeneration when impending blindness threatens? It would be denying the core of their very being.

And how about the people in Christian Science nursing facilities, where no medicine of any kind is used—not even for pain relief? Is everybody attuned to patients who may be suffering? Are they voicing their concerns or holding back, sticking it out because everybody in these places is a Christian Scientist and doesn't want to hear about pain?

I've had private assurances from those with nursing responsibilities in the facilities that they do make it possible for those whose pain is intense to be transferred to hospitals where alternate care is given if they express the desire to do so. I hope they make it not only possible but easy.

But there are factors beyond honest wishes to show how prayer can work in the life of a dedicated Christian that make people go for do-or-die healing.

It is my contention that do-or-die healing has its roots not in the wishes of the leader of the Christian Science movement historically, but in the system of custom established after her death. And too many people may be bound by custom.

The decades after Mary Baker Eddy's death in 1910 saw contentious lawsuits as to which part of the Board structures she left would control the church. The Great Litigation, as it is called, pitted the Christian Science Board of Directors against the Publishing Society for control. The Board of Directors of the Boston Mother Church won the case in 1922, was given control, and went on to direct the church. Their power, therefore, became almost absolute in terms of dictating doctrine and even custom in the churches across the world.

The decades of the early and mid-twentieth-century witnessed the growth of protocols, which would insure the movement would stay as it was at her passing—to safeguard the purity of the church, an understandable goal. But the decline and misunderstanding of church purpose in the present day and age may be traced to a certain body of these protocols, ways of practicing that the founding generation believed ought to be observed.

Some of these protocols were admittedly given by the leader herself: She had established the *Church Manual of The First Church of Christ, Scientist, In Boston Mass.* in 1895 to set limits on how the Mother Church functions and should operate and how branch churches should run themselves. Hundreds of branch churches existed in 1910, and they were established with democratic governments, electing their own readers to read the "joint pastor" *Science and Health* and the Bible and their own boards to decide who should join. They could take in their own members and establish their own criteria; the First Church of Christ, Scientist in Boston would remain independent and function on its own as a "Mother" church, supervising branches in some coordinating activities.

The Manual specified that branch churches should not get together in a town except to plan a joint function, that a "Committee on Publication" should be formed to counter bad publicity about Christian Science, that finances should be sound and reflect "wisdom, economy and brotherly love," that lecturers should travel the country promulgating Christian Science. The Manual contains both procedural and inspirational matters.

Some of the stipulations in the Manual and Mrs. Eddy's other writings implied more than they said, and protocols gradually developed out of them. Thus, since Mrs. Eddy said that Christian Scientists should be married by ordained clergymen, tradition has held that marriages are not performed in Christian Science churches. Until recently, funerals and memorial services have not been held in Christian Science churches. The Manual stipulates that there shall be no special observations of Easter in the churches; until recently we have not decorated churches for special holidays (though the lesson sermons always focus study on the Bible stories of Christmas and Easter). It is inferred that Mrs. Eddy believed that social events held in churches tend to become a central focus of the congregation to the detriment of spiritual growth. But not everything is spelled out; much extrapolation is necessary. And so informal comments by the leader, or statements in other writings than *Science and Health* became protocols of a sort, as well as her explicit statements.

"We worship spiritually only as we cease to worship materially," Mrs. Eddy wrote. The philosophy behind strict reliance on scriptures and its interpretation as the core of the service was that too often the forms of liturgy could replace sincere "conviction" of the Truths of God coming to individual consciousness. But, interestingly the very forms of simplicity of worship came to be in themselves a kind of sacred observation, a de facto liturgy which should not be altered.

Traditions which began in the early days in the actual practice of worship at the Mother Church and behavioral standards stipulated for its members then spread to branches. These protocols were more or less ordained by the Mother Church through four decades when Boston, as it is called, strictly controlled branch churches in the smallest details of operation. Andrew Hartsook, one of the opponents of strong control from church headquarters, has traced through the church's official periodicals the instructions given to branch churches and their members through the 1920s, 30s, 40s and 50s. Matters of dress, behavior at church services, the reading of books about religion and other procedural matters for members of the Mother Church and branch churches, also, were discussed in *The Christian Science Journal*, an organ of the church, and thus became protocols in their own right.

Readers dressed formally for reading in early days. Ushers performed in a reserved and formal way, gesturing to show seating to churchgoers instead of shaking hands in the sanctuary and speaking to them. No food was to be brought or consumed in a church; social meetings, "ladies' circles" and youth meetings were not allowed. (Christian Scientists, obviously feeling the need for such get-togethers, formed ladies' groups such as *The Christian Science Monitor* study groups and organized their children into clubs outside the church buildings.)

Branch churches, particularly, heeded Mrs. Eddy's statement that "it goes without saying that the use of alcohol and tobacco is not in keeping with Christian Science." Branch church regulations, therefore, forbade members from using alcohol and tobacco.

More important in terms of the present decline of the church than these specific protocols, were the implicit and unspoken protocols, established by long tradition and group will, because they impacted and still impact the view of physical healing in the church.

It has been shown that two traditions flowed out of church practice and theology at the time of the leader's death: Christian Science as a bodily healing method and Science as a new, Divinely inspired and deepened version of Christianity. I have maintained that Mrs. Eddy, while still insisting on the healing of sickness as a major and continuing focus of the church, had moved to the position of a broader interpretation of healing for individuals and the world, made possible by the purification of individual consciousness and strong daily Christian practice.

These two schools both continued to mingle in church practice in the four decades after the leader died, but early on the "healing method" school subtly predominated in the group consciousness of branch churches particularly. Possibly this was natural because of the great torrent of healings in the day when the leader was present. Still, it is important to know how the group consciousness, or protocol of healing method, functioned and functions today to understand why the church is in decline because of overemphasis on physical healing.

If you were a Christian Scientist in the 1930s or 40s, into the 1950s, you did not consult doctors—almost never. To say that it was a disgrace in a Christian Science church to seek a physician would be exaggeration—but not far from wrong. Christian Scientists I heard in the 1950s would joke, "They say we don't believe in doctors. Of course we believe in them; they exist. They're not like ghosts. We just don't consult them."

My children grew up in the 50s, 60s and 70s. We lived near an "enclave" community—that is, a community where there is a Christian Science institution. Enclave communities enforce even stricter adherence to the mores—the unspoken protocols which govern group behavior. Christian Scientists know these as schools in the St. Louis area, in Boston, where the Mother Church is located, and in certain West coast communities where Christian Scientists gather in larger numbers than elsewhere.

In the case of our family, it was a northern Michigan school and camp where young people from Christian Science homes, and during this period other people (because they could not get enough Christian Science young people by the 1960s), came to be taught by teachers who were Christian Scientists. There were two strong churches in the area, and by universal consent and the strength of the community will, you did not do certain things:

1. Smoke or drink. This of course caused major problems at Prom time, occasionally for faculty as well as students. Boys will be boys—girls girls. Still, it was a necessary and important rule not

unlike those in other, non-Science boarding schools.

2. Discuss other religions very much even in classes, especially Catholicism. For some reason early Christian Scientists seem to have picked up the general American distrust in the early 20th century of their fellow Christians in the Roman Catholic faith, and vice versa. I suspect many denominational schools are like this.

3. Swing very much outside the generally socially conservative thought bent of the group psyche. This conservatism didn't seem very closely related to the original stream of thinking of C.S.; it had developed as a radical and new-thought religion, and Mrs. Eddy tended to be rather tolerant of the peccadilloes of "mortal mind." She knew that men would err; that was the whole basis for bringing them back to God. As an English teacher, I hired the late Judson Jerome, a poet I had become impressed with at the Vermont Breadloaf Writers' Conference, to come and meet classes and give lectures on Shakespeare. When he discussed the Bard's possible addressing of some of the sonnets to a young man, it caused a scandal on the campus. Nobody seemed to have heard, or read anything about that supposed bisexuality in modern literary criticism. When the school paper printed a publicity picture of him at work at his desk in Antioch College in Yellow Springs, Ohio, I had to airbrush a cigarette out of his hand.

4. Don't talk negative. Cast everything in a positive way, since evil isn't real and we don't want to give it any reality. Say "I have a claim (or belief) of a cold" or don't even mention it as you go around hacking and choking so as to maintain your belief in the kingdom of God's perfection. If it seemed a little excessive at the time, I can attest that there is something to it: A strong denial of the power of evil and sickness to knock you down does work. The positive seems to be an enduring force for harmony in life and the central thesis of Christian Science that we live as perfect reflections of God's goodness does heal bodies. Still, that jargon, a specialized language was characteristic of those days. It is not so pronounced today.

5. Most and especially, you had to rely only on prayer for treat-

ment. Most of the time, this meant a community of very healthy and physically strong people, undaunted by living on the shores of Lake Michigan, where it is cold eight months out of the year and opening the door means being blasted in the face with arctic gales.

Christian Science has proven over a hundred and twenty years that it can produce healthy people and that colds, flu, asthma, and many chronic problems respond favorably and rapidly to strong confidence in God and the goodness of the Universe that Christian Science teaches. Still, there are times when prayers weren't answered—at least by rapid healing. In Christian Science, at that time and in that place, if you needed emergency room treatment, you did it on the sly. It was not to be discussed. You didn't go to fertility doctors if you had trouble conceiving. If you had cancer, you bore it patiently, trying to get healing. Sometimes, seemingly miraculous remissions occurred; sometimes they didn't. It was the "didn't" that got us, and still gets us, into trouble.

Our children grew up relying on their own prayers, and those of their dad and me, and sometimes those of Christian Science practitioners for healing. I believe they think today that ours was a pretty healthy family, but sometimes illnesses didn't get treated fast enough. I think I agree. They grew up strong and self reliant (and Christian) people and of this I am proud, but there are things I'd do differently. I remember one night our youngest son had fallen skiing and broken his leg. He was taken to the hospital by the school and his leg was set, which was what we agreed needed to be done. (An exception is made in Christian Science for broken bones. They may be set by physicians, though many strict adherents would not have bones set in those days. We would have taken him anyway.) But that night he was in pain, and I sat by his bedside praying. I now wish I'd gone out to get pain medication earlier to help him better. I was quick to take our daughter to the hospital for surgery when it appeared she wasn't getting better with what appeared to be appendicitis. None of our children are now active Christian Scientists, part of a generation which has been lost to the church.

Being in an enclave of Christian Scientists wasn't easy when I had that trouble at the end of a pregnancy that I mentioned in an earlier chapter. Out child was born at about seven months, and neither practitioner nor doctors could help her as she struggled for a day and then died of hyaline membrane disease. My husband and I and our children were devastated. We didn't blame God or feel in any other way but very sad—and grateful for each other. Christian Scientists, like other Christians, of course, believe we go on and thus we knew our child was cared for and would mature without our training somewhere beyond our sight. We believed the promises of Jesus. Still, the grief was intense.

The teaching community at the school was, in general, wonderfully supportive, with the one notable exception I've mentioned before, and in that hour of need, I got to know teachers in ways I'd never been able to before. One fellow teacher came and said she'd lost a newborn and deeply sympathized. Other confessed some of their own sad experiences, things I'd never dreamed they were enduring. Like other Christians, these Scientists were experiencing pain and loss, but weren't free to talk about it unless it had been "successfully healed in Christian Science." We were under a code of silence, glossed over sometimes with religious platitudes. "You need to be spiritually strong." "Know the truth and the truth will make you free." "Don't make a reality of evil." But I came to see that those failures, spoken of openly as they were at the time of our trial, had a binding and deepening influence on relationships with these friends. One learns from failures as well as successes, but we as Christian Scientists have not been good at understanding that truth.

Was conforming to the code—the unspoken protocols—prevalent in all the enclaves? I can only speak for the ones I lived in. On the East Coast, there was more freedom to diverge; to speak one's mind both spiritually and humanly. East Coast Christian Scientists tend to be more liberal than Midwestern ones—perhaps more of a political phenomenon than a religious one. Christian

Scientists in the New York area were often Democrats rather than Republicans and led more sophisticated lives culturally and in the business world. The strong emphasis on ethics and living of the Ten Commandments and Beatitudes that C.S. teaches produced highly respected leaders in major corporations like IBM and Procter and Gamble and Equitable Life Assurance, whom I knew. We could use men and women like this today, and some Christian Scientists are still today leading major businesses with their own demanding personal ethics, but the ranks, sadly, are so depleted that we can't produce many leaders.

In the Greenwich, Connecticut, enclave where we taught, Christian Scientists generally felt more free to speak about problems, to diverge from the protocols and to seek alternative healing if they couldn't "demonstrate" Christian healing in their own lives. Some prominent Christian Scientists in the community we lived in had surgery for eye problems that threatened blindness, hospitalization for diabetes and meningitis and the usual setting of broken bones of children. But the protocol against alternative treatment was still strong, enforced by community approbation or fear of possible rejection. A teacher at the school chose to have surgery for a long-time hernia on a trip away from Greenwich during a school vacation, rather than face questions and silent condemnation of his weakness as a Christian Scientist. Probably most of that supposed condemnation was imagined in that place. I never saw such fine Christian lives as those we lived with at the school for Christian Scientists. Christian Science is highly demanding, but it produces exemplary people.

Still, the protocols against—"doctoring" enforce strong feelings—silence which causes suspicion, and I suppose what we can only call fear. I witnessed at that place sudden heart attacks which killed (since we did not have physical exams our teachers did not have warning that there were heart problems), progressive and untreated congestive heart failure, crippling arthritis, hepatitis and AIDS. Students murmured that the ambulances were pulling up far too often in the lane leading to faculty quarters. It was at this

time in the 1980s, that I began to look seriously at the strong prohibition against seeking aid when healing did not occur.

The point needs to be strongly made that these conditions
might have killed under medical treatment too; as we used to say,
"The cemeteries are full of people who aren't Christian Scientists,"
and I did witness the healings of many, many problems, some of
them chronic and supposedly diagnosed as killers. I never grew to
distrust the healing powers of prayer or Christian Science itself; I
just came to wonder whether so many should die so young if there
were options. Their choices were their own, of course, and admirable in terms of spiritual dedication.

Still, one wonders what these deaths accomplished. Was the
blood of the martyrs in this case the seed of the church? Or did it
dismay people beyond our community who knew about it and turn
them from us? And become part of the same trend that is spelling
the demise of the church?

I suppose that Mrs. Eddy's final linking of spiritual growth and
leading of the life of purity which she called the "Christianization
of daily life," to the removal of sin and sickness was in itself a trap
if you didn't look carefully at it. If you can't show improvement
and healing of your conditions (if you stay sick) then you are, of
necessity, something of a spiritual failure. Is there a point in the
silent protocols when you can call it a day? Admit you are still
suffering and for some reason what worked before isn't working?
Go try other means, be it modern medicine, chiropractic medicine, herbal medicine, homeopathy, or whatever you wish? Not
really. There are many choices, but they aren't sanctioned by the
will of the group.

Most branch churches today (not the Mother Church) have
a membership proviso, signed when one joins the church, that an
applicant "has used Christian Science for healing for at least a year."
And the corollary is that you will use it solely in the future if you
wish to be part of the church. No alternatives. Therein lies the
problem. Because times have radically changed.

In the 1870s, 80s and 90s—even up to about 1945—as we

said in the previous chapter, Christian Science was very appealing and drew adherents because it could promise healing when
medicine was known for its often abject failures. Not only could
you be a deeper Christian, but you could get well when medical
science offered no hope. Testimony after testimony from the early
days begins,—"I was given up for dead by the medical doctors and
then I turned to Christian Science." It was a viable, often work-
able alternative well into the twentieth century to the blunders
and inadequacies of an emerging science of medicine which could
cure only about half the cases which came to it.

Heart trouble in 1940? You were going to die, only ameliora-
tive pain medicines and advice about taking it easy could be offered. Cancer at the beginning of the World War II? Operations,
surgery, could physically cut it out. "We think we got it all," the
doctor would inform the patient, wondering if that was indeed true.
Radiation was being tried to get straying cells. Some patients did
get well; most didn't. Arthritis? Aspirin might bring some relief,
but you must expect to cripple around for the rest of your days,
getting worse. No normal life for you. So Christian Science was a
reasonable choice. It did work in many cases. Why not try it? The
people in the churches were touting it as a healing method, lecturers were going around telling of the marvelous healings that did
occur, and one might join the church and find out that you could
learn to deeply practice Christianity with real life satisfaction,
though that wasn't exactly the emphasis.

The healing method people in the Christian Science movement had won in these days (1910-1945) when medical science
was a growing child for a variety of reasons, but the main one was
that Christian Science was "worth a try" when the alternatives
were so bad. All that was about to change.

Chapter Five

Christian Science
and the Medical Revolution

Until about 1945 Christian Science's healing method and medical science stood on relatively equal terms for a person interested solely in physical healing—particularly if the case was serious, potentially fatal. The philosophy among those seeking Christian Science treatment was, "Why not? The surgeons can do nothing for me. And if I die, well, I could have died just as easily and a lot more uncomfortably under a doctor's care."

After World War II medical science began to take giant steps forward in the healing of diseases heretofore believed incurable. Many diseases still carry death sentences: (e.g. Lou Gehrig's Disease, malignant brain and other rapidly growing cancers). But for two major killing diseases medical science has offered increasingly hopeful outcomes, and the discoveries of effective therapeutic treatment for heart disease and cancer have affected not only the lives of millions of formerly hopeless people, but also affected the ability of Christian Science to attract adherents. I hope I will be excused for being quite explicit in my descriptions. We are, after all, looking at the way the world views Christian Science. It is vital to understand just what happened after 1945 in terms of widely publicized and often successful advances in medical history to see what has happened to us.

At the end of World War II physicians at Johns Hopkins Hospital began performing surgery on "blue babies"—infants suffering from congenital heart disease and doomed to die before the age of six. They repaired heart defects caused by certain kinds of congenital problems and, as a result, brought profound hope to thousands of parents, who began to flock to the hospital in Maryland to have surgery for their children. It was the first time malformed hearts could be seriously improved and death sentences reversed.

In 1951 Charles Hufnagel developed a plastic valve to repair an aortic valve and in 1952 John Lewis performed the first successful open-heart surgery. In 1958 the first successful pacemaker allowed a patient to survive for ninety-six days. In 1965 Michael DeBakey implanted mechanical devices to help a diseased heart. The year 1967 saw the first heart transplant by Christian Barnard. These physicians were establishing landmarks in the practice of medicine.

One of the most significant diagnostic/repair techniques was that of heart catheterization, developed in practical form in the mid-fifties. Forssmann, Cournand and Richards received the Nobel Prize in Medicine in 1956 for developing the cardiac catheter, in which a catheter is put into the heart to measure pressure, diagnose and inject dye so that decisions can be made as to how to improve the hearts of patients, sometimes through open heart surgery.

In 1967 both angiography and bypass surgery were introduced; Balloon angioplasty was introduced in 1977.

All of these advances in the hitherto "fatal" diseases of the heart began to change the outlook for heart patients. By the tens of thousands worldwide they began to flock into treatment centers to use these modern techniques, even though the dangers of open-heart surgery were evident, especially in the early days. But treatments which do not involve open-heart surgery have grown increasingly sophisticated, available and effective. In 2001 almost two million angioplasties were performed worldwide, with an increase of 8 percent annually occurring.

The point is that heart disease was, and is still, the number one killer in America, and by 1970 there was clear hope, and medical evidence, that it could be combated—or its effects at least significantly ameliorated successfully by medical science. To go into a heart center of a modern, big-city hospital is to step into a waiting room where fifty to one-hundred people may be waiting to be diagnosed for treatment of their ailing hearts. Many of them are filled with hope; no guarantees, but there is now effective treatment for this plague.

Cancer treatment saw continual improvements from the mid-fifties to the present day with chemotherapy, increasingly sophisticated radiation techniques and early detection procedures and the investigation of genetic causation in certain types of cancer. The person receiving a diagnosis of cancer no longer must inevitably sign a will and prepare to die, though certainly a reliable cure has not been found and horror stories of the failure of medical treatment and the stress and pain of the remedies like chemotherapy continue to show the world that cancer treatment is not as yet perfected through medicine. Still, a cancer diagnosis is no longer a death sentence.

Other dire conditions have found remedies in the medical world. The constant pain of osteoarthritis has been overcome for many with prescription drugs which are taken daily. Ulcers, knees which don't work, kidneys and livers which are not functioning, most gallbladders which are failing, even illnesses in the womb—now have medical remedies. Oral drugs for many forms of diabetes allow sufferers of that former killer the chance to live long and active lives.

Deaths from childbirth, a major killer of women even in Mary Baker Eddy's day, have decreased to the point of insignificance.

So where does this leave Christian Science as the method of choice for would-be seekers of health treatment? It leaves it high and dry if the only appeal of the religion is for physical healing. The healing method adherents in the church, unchanged even with Mrs. Eddy's strong, late injunctions in her career to view her discovery as a broadened view of Christianity which would reform and cleanse the world and heal sin and sickness and overcome death, have found themselves marching down the road leading a parade with no followers. The public is afraid to convert because they believe it will result in risk to life and health. There are good ways to get well that involve less risk.

No need these days to consult the friendly ladies who put their shingles out and their copies of the Bible on the table in their home offices. To the public at large, it's much easier to go to a doctor with a physical problem. The promise that Christian Science offers: that increased spiritual understanding and growth will follow healing through prayer is too abstract an argument to gain many adherents, though it is indeed true.

So medicine has advanced to the point where it becomes the method of choice if Christian Science is perceived as only a healing method. Gone are the tubes into the stomach, high-risk surgery on the kitchen table, and the giving away of possessions as the ordeal of childbirth approaches. People will choose the church of their choice (at least in America) and today they apparently see little reason to choose Christian Science if it's just to heal their physical problems.

Even though unclean hospitals kill 75,000 patients a year through infection, even though thousands of surgeries are performed inappropriately (the wrong limbs cut off), even though physician malpractice suits hit the papers almost monthly alleging terrible behavior on the part of physicians, newspaper articles about Christian Scientists seem to cause more alarm. "These people are crazy and more than that, they're irresponsible," the public grumbles after seeing the sensational stories in the press. And the sad fact is that Christian Scientists feed into the problems themselves by ignoring the charges, succumbing to communal denial, attributing them to malicious influences or "mortal mind," and drawing ever more deeply within themselves. And worst of all, by sometimes doing the very things the articles allege.

Chapter Six

Public Perception: Some of It's True! Are we a cult?

A dding to the real problems caused by misunderstanding of the central thrust of their own movement initiated by Mary Baker Eddy and a refusal to see the problems in the public perception of Christian Scientists' insistence on do-or-die healing, is another challenge. We are also plagued by glaring misinterpretations about our religious beliefs, and we do not seem to know how to answer them in simple ways which others can understand. The misconceptions continue to be cultivated by the same sort of press sensationalizing that bothered the nineteenth century church. A lot of people know very little about Christian Science; a lot more are really wrong about what they think they know. It's important for Christian Scientists to understand these charges so that, as revitalization of the church in the heartland occurs, they can intelligently talk to people in their own communities—head on—about these untruths.

A website reached with the search topic "Cults," which states that it is for "Independent, Fundamental Evangelical Born Again Christians using only the King James Version" has interesting material about Christian Science. One of the lead articles "Why I Left Christian Science" was written in 1906. It's difficult to understand how anyone could take a one-hundred-year-old detailed exegesis of religious theory seriously, since religious practice has changed so much in almost all denominations in a century. An "ex rabbi who became a Christian Science practitioner and teacher" and who left the movement, lists the theological arguments that he has with the teachings of Christian Science. A brief survey will show how out-dated the criticisms appearing on this site are, criticisms which reflect little understanding of the real meaning and practice of Christian Science.

The Atonement: Citing Bible passages on the sacrifice of Jesus's blood as a payment for all, the author argues that Mrs. Eddy's statement, "One sacrifice, however great, is insufficient to pay the debt of sin—the atonement requires constant self-immolation on the sinner's part," (p. 23 S&H) means she denies the atonement. No such thing. Christian Science is not the only liberal Protestant denomination to insist that Jesus' having paid a price in a certain sense for sin implies more than just that one sacrifice—it means our having a part in accepting and living the meaning of that sacrifice. As we have noted in a previous chapter, there is quite a bit of interpretation today in the spectrum of Christian denominations of the meaning of "Washed in the blood" as the old hymn goes—or as the Bible says, "that he might sanctify the people with his own blood." Christian Science is not alone in teaching that the atonement really marks our at-one-ment with God shown in the life and death of Jesus, and must be marked daily in Christian living. It does not deny that Jesus sacrificed for us all on the Cross.

Baptism:

"It ignores the symbolic act of baptism commanded as a mold of doctrine to the Church." Not true. It deepens the symbolic nature of the concept of baptism. Christian Scientists do not engage in immersion or sprinkling, believing that the profound meaning of baptism whether it is by dipping, sprinkling, going into a river or having water poured over the head, is that one is washed clean of sin and ready to stand as a practicing believer, the spiritual child of God's creating. Let any believer choose how he wishes to be cleansed; just focus on the results in life. This, Christian Science teaches, can be either a one-time experience or a daily one, in which one renews commitment to be "born of the spirit." Christian Science is about constant, daily regeneration.

Lord's Supper: "Christian Science ignores the Lord's own

institution of His supper and instead substitutes a 'spiritual break-fast.' " Not so. Both are remembered, especially on "Sacrament" Sundays, when, after having hearing readings on the Last Supper and the Breakfast on shore after the Resurrection, which Mrs. Eddy emphasized, Christian Scientists go to their knees by the church pews and pray for "communion with the One God" in the spirit of those events.

"Christian Science," says the Jewish-Christian critic from the Edwardian Age, "denies the efficacy of prayer but believes in dem-onstrating the mental propositions of its false theories." I don't have the faintest idea of what this criticism means. Christian Scientists pray daily, sometimes as Daniel did three times a day, silently to God, holding up their troubles, asking for guidance, trusting the God who is eternal Spirit and Love to answer their every need and waiting to hear the answers in thought or through events.

The "Prayer of Affirmation" of the Protestant Church is the central worship tool of Christian Scientists: Understanding God's total love and care for all the cosmos as able to meet every need—whether it is for food, clothing, shelter, employment, patience, companionship, schooling, more faith and spiritual understand-ing, healing of relationships or business problems and healing of illness, mental, spiritual or physical. And Christian Scientists are admonished to pray for all mankind, for the establishment of peace both in individual consciousness and for the world.—"Let there be peace on earth and let it begin with me," is the vocal solo often sung in Christian Science churches as well as in almost every other denomination in Christendom. Prayers of thanksgiving and praise are also part of a Christian Scientist's daily observation. Christian Scientists try always to understand and practice the deepest mean-ing of the injunction, "Pray without ceasing."

We as Christian Scientists know the daily prayer Mrs. Eddy wrote and which many Christian Scientists pray daily: "Let the reign of Divine Truth, Life and Love be established in me and rule out of me all sin. And may Thy Word enrich the affections of all mankind and govern them." It speaks for itself about the dedication of Christian Scientists to prayer.

"Mrs. Eddy says that Divine Science, or Christian Science is the Holy Ghost." Not so—at least not solely the Holy Ghost or Spirit. She believed Divine Science was the manifestation of the Holy Spirit but she did not deny other manifestations of this Spirit. She clearly says in the Tenets of the Mother Church, "We acknowledge His Son, One Christ; the Holy Ghost or divine Comforter; and man in God's image and likeness." That is fairly plain.

"Christian Science does not recognize Satan and his hosts as real beings." That is true. Neither do at least half the congregants in whatever sampling of Christian churches across the nation you choose. There is a lot of speculation and interpretation about who, or what Satan is, and Christian Science is not out of the mainstream by believing Satan is evil thought, a lying temptation. It is true that Christian Scientists do not believe that evil or Satan has real, ultimate power. Evil is part of the mortal, material, human world that is not eternal and therefore not ultimately real. God is described as having all power; therefore Satan and evil are ultimately powerless in the face of God's omnipotence. As we are, ultimately perfected after death, in the "heaven" Jesus promised, when we stand as spiritual beings before God after our final purification and ascension so are we in our real selfhood here on earth, perfect, eternal spiritual beings.

Every Sunday, Christian Science services close with two readings. One is from *Science and Health*.

There is no life, truth, intelligence nor substance in matter. All is Infinite Mind and its Infinite manifestation, for God is all in all. Spirit is immortal Truth; matter is mortal error. Spirit is the real and Eternal; matter is the unreal and temporal. Spirit is God and man is his image and likeness. Therefore man is not material, he is spiritual. (Science and Health with Key to the Scriptures)

A powerful, evil being known as Satan is not part of the cosmos of an all-powerful God.

How can we identify ourselves today, the faithful who call Christian Science churches their spiritual home? We are a group of about 70,000 people worldwide, a group that has been fading away month by month since the 1950s, but has recently begun showing signs of revival in the grassroots.

The reformists are a small but important minority, still. I think many Christian Scientists have been "in denial" for as long as anyone can remember, and there aren't good mechanisms for change at the official levels of the church. The signs are good, however that thought is opening.

If I am asked by those outside the faith, I say that my fellow religionists are the most wonderful, dedicated Christians anyone could want to know. In all the professions they serve, which is almost everything except the medical they are the honest brokers, the peacemakers, the office moms and pops, often those who can make a choice for integrity when the chips are down. This is the way they read the Bible.

Their way is hard. Some people respect the Christian Science faith; certainly that was true before the brontosaurus came into the living room after the medical revolution starting in the 1950s. At that time, if in a group you stated your faith as Christian Science, you were greeted with respect. "Everybody I know who's of your faith is really committed to living the religion. And they're trying to be loving, no matter what," would be a typical comment.

Today if you announce you go to the Christian Science church, you are greeted by embarrassed silence many times. In their eyes you can read it: You are the people who insist on suffering unnecessarily.

Still, nobody denies the commitment involved. It's a tough road with a message that has been ringing for members some one-hundred twenty-five years now. If you wish to follow Christ, you need to take his admonitions seriously. Practice Christianity. You, and all the world can be made "every whit whole" by this sort of consecrated practice—which denies the ultimate reality of evil.

The central tool for spiritual growth for us all as Christian

Scientists still remains daily reading of a Bible lesson, together with spiritual exegesis on what the Bible lessons mean from Mrs. Eddy's book *Science and Health with Key to the Scriptures*, the textbook for study of the path to faith.

The book is so saturated with the Bible that it doesn't make complete sense without the Bible. Recently the Mother Church in Boston has been spearheading a major campaign to gear all efforts towards acquainting the public about Christian Science into the selling and giving away of *Science and Health*, and many Christian Scientists, puzzled and dismayed by the decline in their numbers, have enthusiastically signed on for this effort. We are, in my opinion, missing the real point. Becoming a Christian Scientist is not about reading a book, however wonderful. It is about committing to a lifetime of seeking the Allness of God.

Visitors who attend our churches on Sunday still see Christian Science sticking to basics. They still see that the Bible and *Science and Health* are the preachers, using scriptural study subjects delineated long ago by Mary Baker Eddy on topics such as "Love," "Spirit," read. Hymns traditional to Protestantism and some especially written for the denomination are sung with organ accompaniment; a soloist sings, silent prayer and the Lord's Prayer are included. No praise bands, no choir, no dramatic interpretations of the sermon, no TV screens, no announcements of church dinners. This, I suppose, is both bad and good in terms of modern church presentational philosophy; people do love the "selected short subjects." But to immerse yourself as a Christian in a solid hour of quiet communion and focus on the Scriptures and their interpretation is an uplift for the week and life in general. It is, I believe, a marketable commodity.

There is so much to tell the world about the value of these down-to-earth and still up-in-heaven rotating lesson subjects. They allow for the exploration of scores of concepts in the Bible. Lessons are prepared in Boston, but whoever does them works for improving the daily walk by focusing on concepts central to the Christian life. The subject of "Light" is mentioned many times in

Old and New Testament, so the six-part study lesson on "Spirit" may focus on Light. The lesson takes us through from Genesis to Revelation with references to light as a quality of God's person-hood. Grace itself may be the focus of the lesson on Love and ci-tations from both the Bible and *Science and Health* show how grace should be lived in the Christian life. Mrs. Eddy believed that God could be viewed from a sevenfold lens, (instead of just the tradi-tional triune Father, Son and Holy Spirit, which she did not deny). And Bible study groups just originating in homes and our churches today are exploring the deep implications of the Bible and Mrs. Eddy's interpretations of Bible passages. It is a good trend, particu-larly if others in the community can be invited and involved.

We can talk about the discipline these lesson-sermons instill, day after day, year after year in following the Christian way of life and in interpreting it through its radical lens, Christian Science, which insists on unrestricted reliance on God to meet every need.

What can we say are the demands of the theology? Accept God as the all-powerful Creator of the Universe, reject the claims of sin and sickness as impositions on the perfect image and like-ness of God and go out in the world and take care of others in Jesus' name.

It is a cleansing, inspiring way to lead a life—and that's why most of us Christian Scientists choose it when there are hundreds of other ways to worship, and why we want to share this way of regeneration and commitment with the world!

We are as far from culthood in our serious pursuit of Chris-tianity as you can get.

Let's go back to the hundred-year-old list of objections on the website. I'd like to deal with one about which there's a good deal of misunderstanding, or ignorance.

"Mrs. Eddy claims that Christian Science, of which she is the founder, is the [only] Second Coming of Christ." No she doesn't. Christian Scientists believe the Bible. Just as they believe in the Virgin Birth and the Resurrection and Ascension as they are literally described in the Bible, they do not deny that Jesus can come again in a real form onto the earth, but they also believe that Christ comes each day to those who love him as Truth. God permeates the human consciousness, is indeed the only source of true consciousness, and acts for good. That is the Second Coming in a "today" form, and it may be the Third Coming, Fourth Coming and One-hundreth coming in the days of each person's life. "Occupy till I come," Jesus commanded, and Christian Scientists want to be busy living his Truth, reflecting his spirit, as both remembrance of who He was and is, and promise of the conversion of the whole world and the next appearance on Earth—however and whenever that might be.

Implicit in the point just made in the old-time critique is the notion that Mrs. Eddy is worshipped, instead of God, by Christian Scientists. That is one of the classic definitions of a cult: that the leader becomes deified and worshipped instead of the Divine Being and it is one of the problems of perception alluded to in the beginning of the chapter.

I can say emphatically that in fifty years I have never seen anybody worshipping or deifying Mary Baker Eddy. In the years following her lifetime, when some who had seen Mrs. Eddy or were drawn to the church because of her were still alive, there was a lot of overly saccharine describing and praising of the woman. Too often those around her turned her into a plaster saint. To read the series—"We Knew Mary Baker Eddy," written in the years after her death, is to become a little skeptical about the ability of the early students to separate the human person from the spiritual leader. Many will not agree with me on this point, but I do not see any benefit to over adulation of the leader, who stands quite well on her own ground as the brilliant and God-directed woman who has changed the history of Christianity.

One beautiful little pink book with a hand-colored illustration as the frontispiece seems to portray Mrs. Eddy standing in the hall of her elaborate mansion, welcoming all with a halo of goodness around her, unfailingly serene, glowingly beautiful and at all times inspiring. Readings of the modern, well researched biographies of Robert Peel (himself a devoted Christian Scientist) and Dr. Gillian Gill (not of the Christian Science faith) show a leader usually astute and utilizing sound practical management skills consummately to build her church enterprises, often at the pinnacle of prayer and spiritual revelation, but just as often discouraged, frayed and irritated by the dense-headed behavior of her lieutenants, bad food and poor housekeeping at her homes, vicious betrayals by her trusted friends and sub-leaders in the movement, and muck-raking attacks by the press. She was sometimes vain and sometimes ill-tempered. This was a broadly human woman as well as a consecrated Christian religious founder. But some have needed a plaster saint.

It is thus possible to understand why the fallacy got around that Christian Scientists are "worshipping Mary Baker Eddy." At one level it is laughable; at another shocking. Christian Scientists would consider it as blasphemous as other Christians to worship anyone but God.

The Book of Revelation describes a woman "clothed with the sun" with twelve stars for a crown. Some Christian Scientists wanted to connect the dots and show the leader of the new world religion as the woman of prophecy. Did Mrs. Eddy feed into the "She is the woman of Revelation" idea? To read the historical record is to see that she toyed with it. People of remarkable achievements, especially those who have risen from humble beginnings, often are remarkably jealous of their own reputations; humility may come and go for the high achiever. In her case, with constant diatribes from the press and ungrateful excoriations from old friends and relatives after she had "arrived," steeped in metaphysical thought all day long and surrounded by many (and sometimes sycophantic) students and admirers, she might have sometimes thought, "Well, maybe I am some sort of fulfillment of prophecy."

But after this toying with grandiose ideas, she came to believe that nobody could really specify who did, or didn't fulfill prophecy and that she was best assuming, and living, humility instead of believing the sometimes fawning assertions of her friends and followers.

The Mother Church waffled on this subject. In 1943 they seemed to at least acquiesce in the belief that she might be "the woman of prophecy." But in 1991 the Church organization seemed to settle the question definitively when its Board Chairman, Harvey Wood, disavowed the 1943 pamphlet "Mrs. Eddy's Place," which had hinted at exalted status.

Feeding the idea which is really viewed both then and especially now as a heresy in Christian Science—that Mrs. Eddy was some sort of definite fulfillment of prophecy, woman in Revelation, Second Coming type of leader—was a book by a student of hers who had fallen completely under the human spell of his leader. The press avidly picked up this story and as usual did not fully state its scope, implications or final resolution. Ira Knapp was one of Mrs. Eddy's most loyal students in the early days. His son Bliss Knapp wrote a book about Mrs. Eddy's place in prophecy. He spared no horses in hinting at her special place in ecclesiastical history, and his book was not viewed as credible by many Christian Scientists. The Mother Church repudiated it in 1948 because its odd semi-deification seemed blasphemous.

An interesting schism occurred in the recent history of the church because of this book. Bliss Knapp became wealthy, and when his equally wealthy daughters died, his considerable fortune was left to the Mother Church with fall-back legatees of Stamford University and the Los Angeles Museum of Art. Formidable conditions were attached to the bequest to the Mother Church. To receive 93 million dollars, virtually every reading room in the U. S. must agree to receive the Bliss book *The Destiny of the Mother Church*, claiming Mrs. Eddy was the woman of Revelation. Some congregations throughout the country, most of whom had grown quite independent in the thirty years since the Mother Church quit involving itself in their affairs on a day-to-day basis, rebelled. Grass roots Christian Scientists accused the Mother Church of caving to commercial interests and serious financial reverses due to the failure of a 1980s "media empire" that didn't work, and which will be spoken about in a later chapter, of affirming (through acceptance of the book) truths that they knew perfectly well had been long discredited and which Mrs. Eddy herself didn't allow her students to foster.

"You compromise the whole religion if you accept books with such hogwash for money," was the belief of many branch-church Christian Scientists. The Mother Church debated and hedged. They said that they didn't necessarily support the views in the book and that this book was indeed part of a series of books they had decided to sponsor which had "differing views of Mary Baker Eddy."

Many other branch churches viewed the Bliss Knapp matter as a test of loyalty to the Mother Church and simply accepted the books.

But dissenters withdrew their memberships from both branch churches and the Mother Church over the issue. Still, as it is prone to do, time healed most wounds. The books arrived in almost all of the world-wide Christian Science reading rooms. The few people who took the trouble to read the book found the arguments neither very well advanced nor world-shaking, and the books mostly gathered dust on the shelf. The Mother Church collected a large portion of the bequest from the settlement and life went on.

Two fringe groups today continue to emphasize Mrs. Eddy as a sort of saint or sub-Christlike figure. Andrew Hartsook of Zanesville, Ohio, editor of "The Banner," and a thoughtful researcher into the history of Christian Science, regularly criticizes the Board of Directors in Boston for washing its hands of any assertion that Mrs. Eddy is the woman intended in Bible Prophecy. This paper's editorial position seems to be that the decline in membership figures is caused by in improper view of Mrs. Eddy's place in history, plus other misguided administrative procedures and processes.

A publishing company run by a Helen Wright holds the same general position. It is not one accepted by the majority of Christian Scientists.

Mrs. Eddy herself probably made the final statement on the

subject in a private memorandum she dictated to her adopted son Ebenezer Foster Eddy in the early 1890s, when there was a good deal of hubbub about how she, and others should think of her— answer to prophecy or not. Though it has never been published, this is the substance:

To help settle this problem I will once for all silence my sensitiveness and give the definition of my present genus homo, so far as I understand it.

1. In belief, I am a human being and should be treated as such, and spoken of as such, until I find my place outside this state of being.

2: So far as I know myself, and history, I am the discoverer and founder of Christian Science . . . .In the flesh I am not what I desire to be; I am not what imagination would make me. I am not a heathen concept or idol. I am not a personality to which others look and are saved, and the world's present ignorance of the place I occupy should suspend its judgment. I am not the Door through which to enter, nor the Rock whereon to build, but that what God has spoken to this age through me is the way and sure foundation, and no man entereth in any other way into Christian Science. (Robert Peel: *The Years of Trial*, p. 300 quoted in Gill on p. 414).

She did not want herself turned into a heathen idol, what she called a Dagon, and she had ample proofs in her own life as an elderly woman that she could not claim special exemptions from the ills of the flesh.

And that is the generally accepted view of the leader among Christian Scientists: no worshipping of human beings.

But if, as I affirm, as the years have gone along and other Christian denominations have broadened rigid doctrinal assertions about what is basic to the Master's teachings, have reached out in general to enunciate a positive view of Christianity's promise instead of a restrictive one, and if then what was considered radical in Christian Science a hundred and twenty-five years ago is now more in the mainstream of Christian thought, the question can be raised as to what makes Christian Science different?

What can we tell others about why one should choose Christian Science over any other Christian church? The answer is that it is unique in insisting that God is All, matter unreal and that error has no power. Thus man remains the pure and perfect image and likeness of the Creator, and out of these truths all healing in life comes. This is what it has to contribute to the stream of Christian thinking. That was the original, final direction of Mrs. Eddy's revelation and teaching and it is to that stream we need to return.

We have not dealt with the most telling and damaging objection to Christian Science in the public mind. It was not covered in the old list. It is that Christian Scientists endanger the lives of their children, sometimes even allowing them to die. That assertion, the most damaging of all the "bad PR" items alleged against Christian Science deserves a separate chapter.

Chapter Seven

Suffering Children?

Although for years charges have been hurled at Christian Scientists and their church as to the care of children in Christian Science families, that criticism seems to have intensified in the last thirty years, when medical treatment for serious illness has become more systematized and effective. Clearly it plays its part in the decline of the movement.

Christian Scientists early came under criticism for not allowing their children to be vaccinated for smallpox, diphtheria and other childhood diseases. Until about 1970, most Christian Science children did not receive vaccinations unless they were going abroad. The Committee on Publication in various states lobbied legislatures to exempt the children of Christian Scientists from state laws requiring immunization (just as they lobbied to have these children exempted from studying about physiology in school) and many states have exemptions. Freedom of religious choice and freedom from compulsion for views differing from the majority's are the rationale for the legal exemptions.

A serious measles epidemic in the 1980s at a Christian Science school, an epidemic that made several young people dangerously sick and resulted in the death of a student, focused public attention in the public press on a couple of problems connected with the refusal to immunize C.S. young people. Editorial writers commented that it was deplorable that promising young people had to suffer from a disease which had been on the decline because of the measles vaccine. Others worried about the spread of the disease in the population at large (meaning children who did not receive vaccination because they could not afford it or for other reasons) by those who refused to be inoculated and as a result contracted the disease.

Many at the school who did get measles did not die but instead experienced quick or gradual healings using prayer alone, but the implications of even one death viewed as preventable made the public at large critical.

The measles epidemic was one of several cases in the 1980s which made Christian Scientists themselves discuss, perhaps for the first time, the situation of parental responsibility when spiritual means are used for healing.

A notorious case headlined in newspapers around the country was that of Ashley King. A twelve-year-old with bone cancer, she was kept at home with a "problem with her leg" until a concerned teacher and eventually a detective from the police department who had seen the girl raised the alarm. The *Atlantic Monthly* in an article by Caroline Fraser reported Ashley had a huge tumor on her leg, one which was apparently causing her great pain. The girl seemed to be dying, the detective testified. After a court order mandated that she be taken to the hospital, newspapers reported health care providers' shock at the size of the tumor and the pain the girl reported feeling. Doctors who believed she would have had a 40-60 percent chance of surviving had she received earlier treatment, recommended the leg be taken off to spare her pain in the time that remained to her, but the parents took her to a Christian Science nursing facility, where she died.

In the year 1988 there were seven national court cases against individual Christian Scientists, practitioners and the Mother Church itself. Many went on for years with varying results; the Mother Church lost some cases, won others, but the end results were devastating to Christian Science and helped accelerate the negative view about it in the public mind.

In 1990 the Twitchell case gained national notoriety. Ginger and David Twitchell of Hyde Park, a section of Boston, were convicted of involuntary manslaughter in the 1986 death of their two-year-old son Robyn, who had an intestinal blockage which, the prosecution contended, could have been removed by surgery.

To be fair to the Twitchells, they presented testimony that showed their deep concern as parents and their innocence when it came to understanding their child's condition. It should also be said that ninety percent of Christian Scientists in the 1980s wouldn't have waited to seek treatment for a child who seemed dangerously ill. They would have taken any child who was obviously not improving and whose condition seemed serious to a hospital emergency room.

But "most" isn't all. The minority of "bodily healing above all" Christian Scientists who may be viewed as deeply sincere about their religion and who loved their children as much as anybody else, knew of nothing else but to stick to their beliefs—and prayers—sometimes until the end.

But there are two points to be made about these notorious court cases and the general view that Christian Scientists make their children suffer when medical care is available. The first is that the cases cited constitute a telling (and very sad) minority whose very sensationalism causes loss of perspective. We need to get specific about the total deaths of children in America under various kinds of treatment, and the small percentage of deaths of children under Christian Science treatment. There are 10,000 cases per year of bacterial meningitis, about two thirds of them in children, according to an attorney's website on the subject. (Goren, Goren & Harris. P.C) The very fact that a site exists to inform parents that they may be eligible to file a medical malpractice suit suggests that many babies are dying under medical practice. "Delayed diagnosis and treatment of a bacterial meningitis is the most common form of meningitis malpractice claim," according to the website. Children who are not Christian Scientists are dying out there of this awful disease, and sometimes because physicians' care is not fully competent. Anyone with a neighborhood or church circle of friends can attest to woeful or inadequate diagnosis and treatment of diseases for children in the world of medicine.

It is telling to note, and actually a tribute to the effectiveness of spiritual healing that in the article cited in *Atlantic Monthly* by Caroline Fraser titled "Suffering Children and the Christian Science Church," after an extensive search for childhood deaths attributed to Christian Science treatment, only sixty-four cases could be found over a period of some fifty years. (April 1995)

Since the reporter estimated that there were some 5,000 children in the country being brought up under Christian Science care in the 1990s alone, the number seems small. The *Reader's Digest* article "Death Beds" (February 2003) reports that the deaths of 2,610 children in the year 2000 could be attributed to hospital-acquired infections. This is true malfeasance, these deaths truly preventable. Any child, of course, who dies is a tragedy and that children are dying under medical care is no excuse for preventable deaths occurring in Christian Science.

If Christian Science is to survive and grow through the present century, I believe parents who are Christian Scientists and are facing serious illnesses with their children need to be persistent in their prayers, and then if the situation doesn't alter and seems life threatening, they need to look quickly for alternatives. Doctors are not bogeymen; hospitals are not torture chambers and we will all be better off if we can say both to ourselves and to the world at large that we have left no stone unturned in seeking health, and especially life for our children.

Moreover, the Mother Church in Boston needs to clearly enunciate this policy. We out in the field hear that church headquarters says, "Use common sense. C.S. stands for common sense." That's not enough. A clearly stated public policy needs to free church members and adherents of the religion to easily take their children to hospitals and seek physicians' advice if they are faced with life-threatening illness. Old protocols are not at all good in this situation. Beyond that, the Mother Church needs to urge parents to seek responsible treatment when necessary. Nobody wants to join a group for which the public perception is "they let their children die" and that sort of action is morally reprehensible. This criticism should not be interpreted as indicting the very good parents who didn't make the choice for alternative treatment, and who had the tragedy a child's death to live with for the rest of their lives. If we all made it easy to opt for alternatives when illness advanced and didn't yield to prayer, those people might have felt open to choosing. The long-established protocols in our churches against seeking medical help at any time are especially dangerous in the case of children.

Christian Science practitioners, for their part, should not, I think, purport to run young parents' lives. These full-time spiritual leaders, whom Christian Scientists call on to help them through prayer, should do just that and avoid giving "stick to it no matter what" advice. There should be a point where practitioners, whose opinions are so valued by Christian Scientists because they are considered to be (and often are) spiritually advanced, say frankly, "We have reached the point of decision. You are upset and worried and your child doesn't seem to be responding to treatment. I want you to know that you are perfectly free to seek another form of treatment. Above all, this child needs to live." Perhaps they are already doing this; if not, I think they should be.

And what does the Bible say about this, if anything? "You shall not cause your children to pass through the fire to Moloch." The Israelites had an enlightened religion, unlike other nations near them, some of whom believed that first-born children should be sacrificed to the fire within the idol of the god Moloch, so that the nation might be delivered from famine or other plagues. Likewise, we should not allow our children to be sacrificed—even one case where this occurs is too many.

Let me be even more strong in my affirmation, because this matter affects us all and the very future of our beloved church. Those with responsible positions in the church, practitioners and teachers, as well as branch church members themselves, ought to emphasize freedom of choice and parental responsibility instead of parroting church doctrine and reinforcing the silent, stale protocols which govern Christian Science Church groups. Christian Science was born out of radical thinking and individual, moral, choice and these characteristics should be cherished and emphasized.

The horse is already out of the barn on this issue. In the grassroots, the problem is on the way to solving itself. It is the public perception, official church policy, and the few glaring exceptions which need changing. During the 1980s, parents began to talk to each other, and many found they did not, could not and were not subscribing to the extreme viewpoints of do-or-die healing for their children. Probably most Christian Scientists never had. Most Christian Science mothers and fathers found that relying on prayer for healing produced healthy children whose ailments were overcome in a relatively short time. But few children were allowed to go to death's door when healing didn't come after extensive prayer. They were carried to the hospital and medical treatment was sought. And recently that trend has come into the open and is accelerating. So the trend towards totally responsible care of children is happening, though both official policy and public perception have not recognized that fact. It is to the credit of the religion and the reason these people stay on with it that these illnesses are usually quickly healed and the children back playing again. The holistic management of children's health through positive, prayer-directed living without over medication is still the choice of many of us. Many spouses from other traditions come to admire the spiritual way of healing and encourage, rather than discourage it. Spiritual healing and reliance on prayer for family living can and should be a strong point in our future outreach with others on reasons for choosing Christian Science.

Many times young people who have grown up in Christian Science believe it is the best of all ways of practicing Christianity, and wish to continue in it and bring up their own children in the faith. They wish to attract other young people who have grown up without the strong stated and unstated protocols. They are having larger families, obeying the Biblical injunction to "be fruitful and multiply." They wish to do so, and will shape the religion in the next century in their own ways. They will take care of their children, and they will do it logically and responsibly. It is these enthusiastic and sensible people who will shape the future.

Chapter Eight

"It's Your Fault!" "No, it's yours!"

One thing the grassroots revolution will have to overcome is the consistent tendency to blame "Joe." Ever since the 1950s Christian Scientists have blamed each other for the church's decline instead of looking at the simple truth that people didn't need them for physical healing in the way they used to—and that sensational journalism was turning people off, especially focusing on the deaths of children.

Why didn't Christian Scientists see the handwriting on the wall after World War II when the revolution in medicine began to occur? It was the very time when the decline in church membership and new applicants for membership began to surface. Wasn't it easy to sense a correlation between the rise of promising new ways to cure the body of complaints which had plagued the human race as far back as anyone could recall and the fact that people didn't seek out Christian Science for physical healing much any more?

Many may have pondered the relationship in their hearts, but it is difficult to see long-term social trends when one is sitting in the midst of them—amidst pews that were growing progressively more empty.

And there is something about Christian Scientists when they get together which precludes talking about failure "right here in this church—with you and me." Those who look superficially may see Christian Scientists' denial and refusal to face failures, as well as successes as empty-headed, android-like behavior. They miss the point. These people are not dull. Many of us fear that admitting our occasional failure will be denying the all-power of God. This very dedication to uncompromising loyalty is undoing our movement, however. Some of us want to say, "It's OK, it's OK."

There were places where Jesus couldn't convert or heal anybody. One of the places was his own hometown. So if there are missteps, problems, admitting them is the first step towards taking care of them.

And the situation is as serious as it ever needs to get. In 1951 the directors announced at the Annual Meeting that there were 10,503 practitioners worldwide. In a decline that lasted over three decades, by 1982 the July *Christian Science Journal* practitioner section listed only 4,025. The total is much lower now. Church membership, and the actual number of functioning churches decreased at the same drastic rate. Since the mid 1980s over six hundred churches have closed. So we should have known.

But if anyone I knew attributed this accelerating rate of diminishing importance of the Christian Science Church to the fact that other healing options were available, and easier and more reliable at least to the public mind, and that bad publicity had discouraged others from joining the Christian Science church, then I never heard it. It didn't really occur to me in just this way until the last few years. The brontosaurus evidently destroyed everybody's ability to communicate—and think straight—when it came into our living room, or better said, church sanctuary.

Instead, Christian Scientists began fragmenting into groups, each blaming the other for the decline in the church they cared about. Religious groups seem fractious in general, and Christian Scientists particularly confrontational and able to speak their minds.

The tradition to quibble and fight over the Truth is a long and time-honored one among our movement. The church itself was almost destroyed by the original lawsuit between the Board of Directors and the Trustees of the Publishing Society, "The Great

Litigation," which ended in 1922. After that time, the Board, which won the lawsuit, spent much of its time consolidating power in small and larger ways. One of these was refusing to tolerate open criticism, or even discussions, in the field, considering it damaging to the cause and harmful to the advancement of the faith.

Many banked the fires of dissent from 1922 until the 1940s when opposition to the board's controlling strategies broke into open flame. In 1943 a group which took the name Paul Revere began to circulate anonymous letters to practitioners, teachers and anyone really interested accusing the Board of religious autocracy: despotism in the name of theological purity. They gave examples of various Christian Scientists who had tried to send, discuss or have published various unofficial papers about Mrs. Eddy's life. The Board, feeling threatened, pursued the authors of the pamphlets, discovered who they were, and disciplined them.

The issues the Paul Revere group raised were many, and they fueled those who wished to prove that the movement was in trouble because of bad thinking and acting of one sort or another at the Boston administrative level. As the groups surfaced, and circulated their beliefs, which often attacked the Mother Church for its part in the decline of strength of the movement in print, the Mother Church responded by remonstrating against them in print and in person. They demoted them if they held church-approved offices, and condemned them in The *Journal* and *Sentinel* (in ways, however, which avoided naming names) but often excommunicated them.

Many of the protestors were prominent Christian Scientists whose credentials reached back to the time of Mrs. Eddy. Some became the founders of splinter movements which tried to interpret the decline in the movement to specific non-performance causes.

John Doorly's history in the 1920s and 1930s is informative. It illustrates our "ostrich in the sand" mentality which ignored practical conditions in the outside world. Doorly and his followers were among the first who refused to address shortcomings in the practice of the religion and the negative perception in the minds of potential converts. They were the first to advocate "turning inward" to "rediscover the true path of Christian Science." They split off, and the results diminished the number of the faithful and let the press have a field day, a pattern which was to become all too common.

A native of England, Doorly had been president of the Mother Church during part of the Great Litigation. He had been a popular lecturer in the 20s. Turning from Mrs. Eddy's unwavering insistence on "the simplicity which is in Christ"—the practice of the Master's teaching in daily life to bring about healing—he took a more mystical approach. Analyzing the leader's textbook, he believed he found in it a sort of cryptographic secret matrix which revealed the hidden meaning of the universe. He began to teach that Mrs. Eddy's book revealed a system based on the seven synonyms for God that she found in the Bible (God as Life, God as Principle, God as Love, God as Truth, Mind, Spirit and Soul.)

He was a teacher of Christian Science, and therefore had students who would follow his lead into what seemed to some a belief akin to the ancient Christian heresy of Gnosticism. Jesus seemed unimportant, God reduced to an abstract "principle" like the Deists' clockmaker and unimportant in changing human lives. Even Mrs. Eddy as a spiritual leader paled before the study of the secrets of the universe hidden in the pages and chapter heads of the textbook.

Doorly's writings were circulated. People who became his followers met in homes, immersed themselves in the study of certain passages in the book, assembled charts which connected the seven synonyms with the seven days of creation, and seemed to some other Christian Scientists not to care about the daily walk in the footsteps of Christ.

Doorly was excommunicated in 1946. After his death in 1950, his mantle fell on the late Max Kappler, one of his students. The books Doorly wrote were published and his work furthered by what became the Kappler Institute. Today the group, comprised of a few hundred people, still meet to study what is now called "Cybernetic law" found in *Science and Health*. They insist that declining numbers in the church reflect "superficiality in the church hierarchy and the refusal to be Absolute."

Another influential schismatic group in the 1920s was one led by Alice Orgain. She too found hidden cryptography in *Science and Health* based on the twelve tribes of Israel, published a book about it, and incurred the ire of the Board of Directors in Boston. She also insisted, along with her followers, a group important in opinion but not numbers, that the fact that the stipulations in the church Manual, requiring that Mrs. Eddy's signature was necessary for several kinds of business at the time, operated in the present. Thus it negated most of the authority of the Board of Trustees and the Trustees of the Publishing Society.

The Board did not allow this interpretation of the Manual to stand because it challenged their very existence and the day-to-day operation of the movement, so it answered her charges. She was not allowed to function as a practitioner and was excommunicated in 1930. A small, strongly vocal group in the Christian Science movement today still follows the teaching of Alice Orgain. This group, which offers its own books distributed outside official channels, insists that the present decline in the movement is caused by the Board's refusal to honor the "estoppel" clause written long ago in the Church Manual but contradicted by the word of Mrs. Eddy when she established the church organization.

Most interesting is the "Place of Mrs. Eddy" group mentioned earlier which believes wholeheartedly that the decline in the influence of the church is caused by refusing to believe the officially discredited view stated earlier: that "Mrs. Eddy is the woman of Prophecy." They steadfastly maintain that if the church took the official position that Mrs. Eddy was indeed the woman prophesied in the Book of Revelation, that the movement would revive. Andrew Hartsook, the editor of "The Banner" newsletter and the intelligently researched book *Christian Science After 1910*, also states on the back cover of that book, "It is obvious that the main

cause for the present crisis in the movement is not due to circumstances or world resistance to Christian Science, but almost en-
tirely to the despotic control of Directors who disobeyed the
Church Manual and abused the position entrusted to them to such
an extent as to threaten the very survival of the church."

The attacks on the Boston organization have not been con-
fined to groups who transmit their views through books printed,
reprinted and distributed by small publishing companies owned by
Christian Scientists, and through Hartsook's periodically distributed newsletter, which many read. Several individuals seem to have
felt impelled to release sensational exposes to members of the
church and the media. These exposes, delivered in the form of
general letters to churches and their members during the 1970s
and 80s, have helped to spread the impression in the public mind
that the Boston headquarters is an overgrown bureaucracy oper-
ating like some Byzantine court, with intrigues, moral corruption,
the appropriating of funds belonging to widows and orphans, heavy
handed pressure tactics against enemies and abrupt removals of
those who objected to all of this. Mishandling of funds during the
1960s and 1970s was one of the major charges and it has resurfaced
again in 2004.

A new church center several stories high in Boston was being built in the early 1970s. An outside consultant on security, a
Christian Scientist named Reginald Kerry, who had been a fire and
police commissioner, conducted a security survey for the Mother
Church and found, as he traveled around through the beehive of
activity at the church center, that much was amiss. In 1975 he
began a series of "Kerry letters" to the field, in which in rather
overwrought language he sought to show several kinds of misman-
agement, stonewalling and intimidation of critics. He felt threatened, but he kept the notorious letters coming. Unhappy about
the departures of the church from "Christian morality" and com-
plaining of other things, First Church of Plainfield, New Jersey took
steps which resulted in its being ejected from the official Christian Science movement and founded its own mini-movement—

one church.

The new church center in Boston, adjacent to the original Mother church and the larger, newer extension, was an impressive high-rise office building to handle the affairs of the international operation. It was built and dedicated amidst continuing charges that it had cost far too much and that shenanigans had gone into the bidding process.

Harvey Wood became the focus of the charges of unbridled spending and change for change's sake as he became chairman of the Board of Directors. Wood had joined the Board in 1977 and eventually became its chairman. For some time the church had tried to respond to the pressing need for change in the limiting behavioral protocols, the declining church membership and the readership of the distinguished newspaper *The Christian Science Monitor*.

In September of 1988 under Wood's direction, World Monitor television programming premiered on the Discovery Channel. It was followed by the funding of a magazine and more heavy investment in electronic media, including the twenty-four hour Monitor channel, March 1991. By April of that year *The Washington Post* was reporting that media losses for the church over two years had totaled more than $100 million. Much money, a good deal of it invested funds from older church members who had left their estates to the Mother Church, had been wasted and would never be recouped.

This period in the 1970s, 80s and early 90s, the letter-writing, charges and counter charges, accusations, hateful talk and the resorting to lawsuits seems to have reflected a sort of hysterical reaction to downhill change more than anything else. Grieving brought on a bitter irritability. It was a cannibalizing and splintering similar to the sort of arguing that occurs when a family or nation is beset by unhappy factors it can't understand or seem to do much about over a rather extended period. One thinks of the anger mixed with the love and devotion of those who must render long-term care to invalids they love. Sisters and brothers can turn against each other in such a time.

Some would call the splintering stress-related. The religion Christian Scientists loved seemed to be slowly dying, and the true reason—that physical healing was getting easier for people in medical offices than in the church—and that people were driven away in the face of growing public criticism when our members died under Christian Science care—couldn't be faced. Another truth—that those who cared needed to dig deeper than "healing method" and offer people the spiritual essence of the faith—was too hard to think about. So they blamed each other. It was not a very good way to move forward.

It is an easy thing to blame the people "at the top." Everything that goes awry in America is the result of the President. American Catholics blame "The Vatican" for not acting to stop the sexual scandals in the priesthood and for the decline in priests and nuns choosing a vocation—and for everything else they can think of that is going wrong. And the decline of Christian Science is thus attributable to whatever scandal it is that is supposedly going on at the Mother Church.

It seems to me "Boston" does not need to take on extra blame. There are enough current problems, especially financial, at the Mother Church, to keep the leaders there occupied for quite a while.

A Visit to The Mother Church Today

Since those of us in the heartland have been left virtually alone by the Mother Church for over twenty years, as they concentrated on their own challenges and implemented a decision to let the democratic branches stand on their own, a visit to the huge church headquarters in Boston seems an almost foreign experience. The country mouse has come to the city, and the view is certainly impressive. Mrs. Eddy's relatively small first church, with its stained glass windows and turrets, sits nestled now among tall limestone office buildings, and a large and new Sunday School building. Most recent among the additions is the completely re-done 1930s Publishing Society building which has become the Mary Baker Eddy Library for the Betterment of Humanity. This new public library, which is on "stops" for tour buses of Boston, has a room of spinning, electronic versions of the world map, light shows of the quotations of the world's children who wish for peace and happiness for all the world, and a trendy, art deco café named Quotes. Mrs. Eddy's correspondence and all her writing are now available to the public on upper floors, along with thousands of books on spiritual living and healing. Life has gone on at the Mother Church; decay is not obvious here. Only recent firings of some top officials and discouraging financial statements show a hidden trend here, too.

The large, refurbished main church edifice still leads to the beautiful, domed sanctuary where Christian Scientists from around the world can come to worship, and attend the vital meetings of the Annual Meeting for all members in early June. Warm welcomes to visitors and changes toward informality make the services seem forward-thinking. The awe-inspiring organ rings with traditional hymns enthusiastically sung. There is plenty of room for visitors, and they seem to be present.

Financial records show the asset value of the Mother Church's holdings has fallen between 2002 to 2003 by about 8 per cent. The Ernst and Young audit shows continuing substantial income of $60 million, but growing expenses which exceed income. Assets are being used to cover a significant shortfall of $90 million. Other not-for-profit organizations, of course, have been experiencing shortfalls during the period of a recession economy, but even more recent figures show serious problems.

In 2004 serious charges of accounting errors have compounded the difficulties.

"What do they do in those buildings?" some of us in the heartland wonder. "We're not a very large denomination for such a large facility." We know of course that people in the buildings direct practitioners and lecturers and certify new churches and missionary work around the world, which is significant in Africa, particularly. They oversee *The Christian Science Monitor* and other publications, radio shows and electronic (internet) outreach activities, all of which are of excellent quality. They prepare the weekly lesson sermons and generally set directions for the church and plan for conferences which try to improve reading rooms and Sunday schools. Their activities are probably not much different from those of other denominational headquarters.

The message of Christian Science is still alive and well, for those of us who do accept it and for others who will come. No one of us who cares about spiritual revitalization and spiritual healing of the ills of mankind doubts that. It is just redirecting that message for the future and that job does not, in large part, fall to the people here, but to those of us in the cities and towns beyond Boston.

No, it is not the Mother Church that primarily causes the denomination's problems. "We have met the enemy and it is us," as the comic strip character Pogo so aptly commented. We as Christian Scientists have had enough of ostrich mentality in the past to serve ostrich filet mignon to many fine gourmet restaurants in the country, and that needs to be put aside if we wish revitalization of the movement.

Still, it is not as if local churches have not addressed the problem of declining interest and membership. We believe in what we have and wish sincerely to share it. Besides, that is the Gospel admonition: Go into the world, heal the sick, raise the dead, cleanse the lepers, freely you have received freely give. We wish to do just that.

When we can get people in the doors of our branch churches, they stay, appreciating the peace of mind that both the service and the way of life bring. But new people don't come. Christian Scientists, like other declining denominations, have study groups and prayer meetings to try to figure out why. We talk about renting space on buses at great expense to advertise Mrs. Eddy's book *Science and Health*. As we discuss declining membership, we ignore the totally obvious and irrefutable facts that form the basis of the argument in this book. People don't join us because they believe they will have to die or forgo basic medical treatment if they can't "become a better person" and remain sick. If we don't do something about that perception, nothing else will work.

How many people will die for their faith in this way? Depending on the generation involved (older adherents are much more likely to tough it out to the death) about 20 percent. It is this percentage that gets into the critical books and magazine articles.

And added to the perception that people die before their time is the knowledge of celebrities who have been in the public eye and about whom people say, "She was a Christian Scientist and they have to die if they get really sick. They refuse medical help."

In the 1950s, Christian Scientists proudly pointed to their celebrity converts who had attracted public notice with articles in movie magazines and newspapers. "Doris Day is a Christian Scientist," church members would say. "She was in *Look Magazine* talking about her faith." Then things went sour and the public noticed that, too. Doris' husband Marty Melcher, described as a "devoted Christian Scientist," was reported to have convinced Doris that she did not need to seek medical attention even though she was suffering from an internal cyst. She was willing to go along with Christian Science treatment for a period of three years; finally the situation approached emergency status and she was rushed to the hospital for a hysterectomy. She could have no more children.

Marty himself succumbed to a lingering illness, still refusing treatment. Both fan and news magazines dwelt on the sad details: nursing care required, gradual wasting away while medical treatment was refused, final deathbed scene. The entire situation was disheartening and sad.

Thousands of testimonies of healing, many of conditions diagnosed by physicians, were reported on in publications like *The Christian Science Journal* during the 1950s and 60s, but Doris Day's conversion to Christian Science is still being cited (sometimes by Doris herself, admittedly) with avid intensity as a sad mistake in judgment which led to tragedy.

What's the point of the celebrity examples? That the press, always intensely interested in things that don't succeed as they had since the religion's earliest days, picked up on the failures of Christian Science and ignored the good that was benefiting thousands of people. People will be people, however, and it is in the public eye, by word of mouth, that people are attracted to the churches of their choice—or not. The contrasts with medical science's triumphs were often stressed after 1950. The small voice which could tell of a truly helpful way of understanding God was drowned out after 1950 by a flood of bad press—the reporting of what was deemed by the public unnecessary suffering and dreary death before man's time.

During the 1950s, 60s, 70s, and 80s I was myself healed of the following conditions: trenchmouth, stomach ulcer, effects of a miscarriage, flu, continuing heart palpitations and pain, gallstone attacks and a broken bone in the back (T-16.)badly sprained wrists and knees. Colds which had been a problem before I turned to Christian Science, became quite rare in my life, flu nonexistent.

I also had a hysterectomy under conditions of semi-emergency and found I could not talk about it to my fellow church members. They—all of us—were interested in the triumphs and successes, but unwilling to deal with the failures of faith when it came to bodily healing.

Chapter Nine

Into The Future

Christian Science stands today at the portal of a promising new age. In the world, the movement of thought is in the direction Mary Baker Eddy encouraged for Christians who wanted to emulate the Master: the practice of spiritual means to heal bodies, minds and spirits. Her own evolution as a Christian thinker from the beginnings of her spiritual practice in the 1860s through the first decade of the twentieth century stands as the basis of the religion today: God as all powerful good, to be worshiped and understood as the basis of all existence and matter and all its pull as irrelevant, temporal. Man as God's full image and likeness.

From many sides comes news of interest in healing through prayer: a survey in California finds that hospital patients who had prayer offered for them seem to improve faster and better than those who don't. Methodists, Catholics, Episcopalians, Presbyterians are scheduling healing services which may or may not include the laying on of hands. Universities gather those from many disciplines and segments of the scientific community to study how Spirit influences the body and mind and changes things. Doctors themselves gather to pray, and many ask their patients if they wish prayer included in their treatment. Thousands can testify that in some way, possibly unexplainable to them, possibly perfectly obvious, they have experienced healing of so-called terminal diseases, life-threatening medical crises, seemingly impossible physical situations. And most Americans believe that prayer can change things, solve quandaries which seemingly are impossible.

Some of my friends ask what actually occurs in spiritual healing. "Does a person wishing healing concentrate or get outside himself when seeking to be healed?" I do not profess to be a spokesman who can answer this question definitively. I can only say that when I badly wrenched my arm so that all feeling left it (I had to drive one-handed) and the effects were still around two months later as pain and stiffness, I became meditative one afternoon. I just turned to God, feeling myself one with Him. A feeling of total love and assurance came over me and I felt the pain and stiffness begin to ebb away, like water draining out of a sink. The pain and stiffness were gone. Other times prayer must be more consistent to get a desired result. And one mustn't forget the therapeutic benefits of trusting God for health. The mental climate established by prayer and meditation seem to constitute real, measurable protection against disease.

Yes, healing is a primary focus for us and always will be. But I contend again that Christian Science is no mere healing method, in spite of the sometimes superficial versions of it being offered by those who want to make it easy to accept, palatable to the generation of easy fixes and overnight miracles. Its validity depends on deep study of the Bible and the interpretive textbook Mrs. Eddy penned to shed light on the practice of total-immersion Christianity. It is a way of life.

Mrs. Eddy arrived at that conclusion some one hundred years ago. And I think a certain strong percentage of Christian Scientists know this. Allison Phinney, Jr., a chief editor of publications for the Christian Science movement, wrote in an editorial in the *Sentinel* in 1984, "Christian Science, contrary to recent public misrepresentations, is not positive thinking, mind cure, or an alternative health care system. It is a profoundly Christian denomination, with its priority on the worship of God and the living of a Christian life."

And if that is so, and it is a Christian path far beyond the issues of whether one takes an aspirin or gets radiation treatment for a tumor, then it can perfectly well afford to give its members the clear option of medical treatment if they are gravely ill and unable to be healed through prayer.

How can Christian Science survive through another century? Can anything staunch the diminution of its ranks, the closing of its churches? Is it doomed to be just another footnote in the history of religion? The answer is NO. It can survive, if those whose responsibility it is, that's all of us who want to see their religious path of life move into the future—do their job, encouraging and expediting change.

Examining outworn protocols is the first step in opening thought to change in any field. The Mother Church, the First Church of Christ, Scientist in Boston has been moving away from protocol and radical conservatism for about twenty years. Many Christian Scientists date the Boston efforts at modernization to the aforementioned board chairmanship of Harvey Wood in the early 1980s and they do not view all of the changes as good. Conservative religionist complained when *The Christian Science Monitor* was "updated" in the 70s with most religious-oriented material being removed, the size diminished to effect cost savings and a generally liberal political point of view encouraged. Millions of dollars had to be poured into the previously described television effort which failed, and periodicals began what some would call a slide towards modernization, with new graphic looks, inclusion of articles not strictly about Christian Science and a wide reporting of "spiritually-oriented" news. What were really breaking up were the old protocols from the 1920s, 30s and 40s, and these were not really the crux of the religious practice and belief instituted by Mary Baker Eddy. That does not mean the denomination should move into extremes—into embracing any belief system, no matter how bizarre or unrelated to Christianity—which claims "spirituality." That is a large word, and it is being abused in its modern context. The tangent the Mother Church is presently on, the "mass marketing" of *Science and Health* and the courting of strange bedfellows like spiritualists, psychics and mind-body personalities in official publications—in the name of showing we share beliefs—will not last forever.

The trend away from old protocols will continue. The Mother Church has paved the way. Readers for Sunday morning services sit among the congregation until the service starts, instead of coming out of the old, lofty doors, emphasizing the democracy of our denomination. Men who are chosen to be readers conduct Wednesday evening services in sportshirts and speak informally to those in attendance. Women are equally informal. Flowers and decorations bank the church at holiday seasons. Friendly announcements, common in Protestant churches but not included in services in the past, have become common in the Mother Church. Recently the First Reader at the Mother Church suggested from the desk that those at the service consider attending the—"Quotes" café in the new Mary Baker Eddy Library. The reader praised the chocolate cake. That sort of affability and departure from explicit and rigid order of the service was unheard of before about 1995. The Mother Church is urging churches through its publications to consider change. Even the King James version of the Bible may be replaced or used as an option; its use is not specified in the *Church Manual of the First Church of Christ Scientist, in Boston, Mass.* by Mary Baker Eddy.

The old jargon is out. Christian Scientists no longer talk about "beliefs" instead of illnesses. People now can be described as dead, instead of "passed on," even though we believe they are existing in the next phase of life, beyond, never having really died.

Other changes are originating in the Mother Church's way of directing its own operations, and advising those in branch churches when they ask. Christian Scientist children have been taught basic scriptural lessons (beginning with the Ten Commandments and Beatitudes) in Sunday schools. They did not color the usual pictures of Jesus with crayons or form animals for Noah's Ark from clay. At a recent workshop for Sunday School superintendents at the Mother Church, teachers were encouraged to use traditional Protestant church Sunday School tools to teach the children: puppets, drama, art and even computer games.

Food has never been served in Christian Science churches; at this workshop refreshments were served to the superintendents. Other Christian churches thirty or forty years ago began applauding musicians in church services; Christian Scientists are now encouraged to appropriately applaud for musical solos and organ music. Window dressing perhaps, but symbolic of change.

But it is in the branch churches across America that real change must happen and is occurring, thankfully.

After all, the Mother Church is a long way away and the branch churches are, in effect, on their own. The vitality one sees in several small but active Christian Science congregations around the nation, the grassroots revolution, shows that many young people value the spiritual commitment that has to be made to trust God completely. Their enthusiasm can be the definitive factor in revitalizing the movement.

Examining outworn protocols is the first step in opening thought to change in any field. I have known of the following protocol changes, which are accelerating in branch churches. I am not advocating all these changes, simply saying they represent a trend of self-examination and willingness to look at new ways which is positive. A church in Florida has allowed funeral services, long prohibited in Christian Science churches, for its elderly members in the church itself. Christmas hymn sings and decorations have been increasing in popularity in the heartland, and some churches are giving children appropriate gifts. Christian Scientists have long had only piano or organ accompaniment for the solos and hymns in the church. Within the last two or three years, instrumental music, including trumpet solos, flutes, percussion instruments and guitars are appearing at special Christian Science services. Food is being served for some types of meetings in the churches themselves.

These movements toward a more liberal church service and use of church buildings have not been without their critics, sometimes strong. Many point to Mrs. Eddy's injunctions against the materializing of worship. She instituted stipulated forms of religious practice in the churches, the argument goes, because she did not wish her churches to fall into the traps of church potluck suppers or the organized wedding business. She wished the focus strictly on the practice of Christ's Christianity. That point is worth remembering as the doors open wider.

Perhaps the most radical change came about in 2003 when the Mother Church allowed its *Journal* to publish a practitioner's article, "What? Me Inflexible?" and Christian Scientists everywhere commented on changes that seem to be inevitable. Among other things the article states:

I rejoice in the new freedom people have to join The Church of Christ, Scientist, even if they aren't perfect. Today a church membership form can be obtained over the Internet. There aren't any questions about smoking, drinking, drugs. Perhaps some members are shocked or think that standards have fallen. But this point of view may need to change, to be more open to the freshness pouring forth from divine Love, who created everyone. . . . When Science and Health is read understandingly, drinking, smoking, use of illegal drugs and immorality will probably drop away.

Those striving for old ways remind the "new thought" people in Boston that in the *First Church of Christ Scientist and Miscellany* Mrs. Eddy stated "Christian Science teaches: Owe no man; be temperate; abstain from alcohol and tobacco; be honest, just and pure, cast out evil and heal the sick; in short, do unto others as ye would have others do to you." So there are dissenting opinions here.

A recent call to the *Journal* editor, inquiring whether the referenced article reflected the view of the church, was informed that it did. "You can call the clerk to confirm that, but basically we over here believe those sorts of things are between a person and God."

Perhaps there are other factors in the Mother Church's attitude towards smoking and drinking. Leading officials of the church, board members in the branch churches and anybody else who cared to, have flouted particularly the social drinking prohibition for years. Probably this private flouting has gone on since the creation of the church. That does not mean that a majority of Christian Scientists have not believed Mrs. Eddy when she said that alcohol and tobacco were not in keeping with the religion. They have, and have found abstinence from smoking and drinking has aided their spiritual growth. But it is beginning to be viewed as a desired goal, not a prohibition for inclusion in the church. And, in spite of the hypocrisy involved, ultimately this has to be a breath of fresh air.

But the implications of these steps is obvious. If even illegal drugs do not constitute an impediment for acceptance in the Christian Science church, then logic demands that by extension those poor souls crippled with arthritis in the congregation, and wishing to have fellowship in the church of their choice, who choose to use Celebrex or Vioxx can also seek, or continue in their membership. And those who are thinking of surgery and chemotherapy for large cancers on their bodies after their own prayers haven't brought relief after months or years of work can rest easy. Go get it cleared up and move on in practising the faith, the Mother Church's stance seems to imply. Pilgrim, "this matter is between you and God."

Bylaws are being changed with restrictive elements such as a year of reliance on Christian Science removed; some societies and churches simply state in essence, "If you wish to pursue the path of Christian Science and learn its special gift of spiritual healing, join us."

In this wide spectrum of belief one thing is obvious: The times are changing and the old protocols are on the way to being largely swept away. What is the sense of being secretive and aloof from the public and other Christians when the membership is small and struggling? Who can afford to observe the old, diffident formalities when the congregation is twenty or thirty people?

If change occurs in branch churches, meaningful change, will everything go—baby with bathwater, as some believe? I think not.

What will remain? What remains for the "healthy remnant," which constitutes the church, I think, are the teachings of Mary Baker Eddy, carefully committed to writing in not only *Science and Health* but also several other books, their own faith in the Master's way, able to be practiced in daily life, and the independence which comes from living, and surviving, mostly away from central authority and dependent only on their own prayers and good consciences and the support of others like them, who become in the small churches good friends, closer than kin? What remains is a good future, if change becomes as valued as it was in the early days of the religion.

Like the outposts of the Roman Empire in 400 A.D. when troops had been called home to defend Rome and the little outposts on the fringes were left to fend for themselves, branch churches are governing themselves more decidedly than ever before. And they are spearheading a renaissance that may stay the decline of Christian Science and bring promise of revitalization. Like Molly Brown, we may be singing, "I ain't done yet!"

And so we come to the matter of survival in the twenty-first century. My calls to action based on the arguments in this book are:

First and foremost, put to rest this suffering children matter. Christian Scientists need to be extremely alert with children. If a child isn't getting healed, parents should take that child for medical consultation and get aid in deciding if medical treatment will help save the child.

Even more importantly for both themselves and the public mind, we must publicly let it be known that Christian Science children should not and will not be allowed to suffer with sickness. If not speedily healed, Christian Science parents will seek alternative means of getting well. This pronouncement must come from the top, from the headquarters in Boston, but if it does not, individual branch churches must make it perfectly clear in ways that will be publicly understood.

The Mother Church must clearly state, and frequently restate, that parents following Christian Science care are free, and indeed are morally (and in some cases legally) obligated, to seek medical care for their children if they are seriously ill over a period of time. When our officials go on television or make personal appearances, they must enunciate a clear and unequivocal policy about children and not hedge.

Christian Science churches and their members must be open to change of non-vital aspects in the way they function, so long as they don't violate the basic tenets or Manual of the Mother Church. The winds of change are blowing, and we must put our faces out the window and explore what they are trying to tell us. Everything must be on the table, the Manual and *Science and Health* and the Bible as our guides, not outworn custom and "community protocols."

The children from Christian Science families who have left the faith, adults who have joined other Protestant denominations and want something more radical, newcomers drawn by the loving commitment of business associates they come in contact with, come to the newly vital branch churches as described above, excited about the possibilities of a life lived to demonstrate the Master's total faith in God and his triumph over every material circumstance. There is no appeal for them in old, out-dated formalisms which are the result of custom only.

Some forward thinking branch churches seem to grow weekly, with regular attendees now outnumbering the members. Members ask themselves—why aren't these regular attendees becoming members? They are coming to the conclusion that it is because these people may still smoke, have an occasional glass of wine or want to feel free to consult a physician if their own prayers do not bring them immediate relief from sickness. The regular attendees believe they can't join our churches under these circumstances.

We must let them know clearly that they do not have to be perfect; certainly those of us already on the membership rolls "haven't walked on water yet." And we must be open, open to God's direction, not stale custom.

In addition, Christian Scientists need to quit brushing aside criticism of their religion as attacks of negative thinking, not to be seriously considered. They need to the greatest extent possible lead the kind of lives that will cancel out the bad public impressions and bad press and attract new members and generate their own positive publicity. And they need to search out what is attractive in their faith and share it.

Christian Scientists recently have tried an initiative to "put a book in everybody's hand," expecting that is enough to explain Christian Science by selling, or handing people *Science and Health With Key to the Scriptures*. *Science and Health*, like most intense theological treatises, especially those written a hundred years ago, is not an "easy read" to be put in the same categories as self-help best sellers. It needs studying, understanding, support from a church community. The personal testimony of individual Christian Scientists about the meaning of everything we've come to find in this discipline is what we need to share, with love which will open doors. The book will follow.

We need to put into universal practice policies which will eliminate both in practice and public perception the idea that adherents to Christian Science suffer and die unnecessarily. Christianity offers the greatest of all rewards to the believer: salvation and eternal life. What does its branch Christian Science offer? Right now pretty scary prohibitions and punishments hardly designed to fill the pews. Let the promises of full spiritual life and healing of body, mind and spirit be the central message the movement promotes: both collectively and individually. Abandon the false notion that people seek us for physical healing and promulgate the Larger Truth. Profess, and practice the fundamental policy that permits adherents to have a choice when healing of physical conditions must be considered.

When the real meaning of the faith which Mrs. Eddy intended is uncovered—again the promises are great: Lives of great peace in surrendering to the good God of Love who is also infinite. The ability to live a life of freedom and purity in accordance with God's commandments will come. Let's be even more specific.

In my opinion, the church at an official level must announce that just as alcohol and tobacco are no longer immediate impediments to membership in a Christian Science Church, neither is resorting to traditional medical practice a bar to membership. Progress is the Law of God. Christian healing should be a goal, a crowning achievement, and not an ultimate requirement for membership. Christian Scientists should learn, teach, strive for and practice spiritual living and healing but they should not compel it.

Compulsion, whether through bylaws or group will and social pressures, dilutes the spirit of Christian charity in a group and makes our denomination seem irrational in punishing those who cannot succeed in its lofty and admirable precepts. We do not throw out or condemn (any more at least) those in our churches who fall victim to fits of lust and cohabit outside marriage. How much less should we put spoken or unspoken condemnation on those who visit physicians' offices to get help for chronic and unhealed problems.

In fact, we should openly allow and acknowledge that it is going to happen, that turning away from the traditional prohibitions is indeed commonplace for many Christian Scientists already. That sitting among us, in our churches, faithful every Sunday, and loving our services and admirably practicing our beliefs, are former readers who use daily medication for pain relief, Sunday School teachers who have had successful surgery for breast cancer, board members who receive insulin daily for diabetes. Why are they there if Christian Science is only a method of bodily healing?

They realize it for what it is: a deeply Christian way of life which is infinitely satisfying because it denies all claims of evil and trusts all in the daily walk to God. Physical healing? Yes, of course, highly desirable and worthy of practice and achievement, though not required to stay in the pews or even join the church.

We are in the midst of a mellowing process, well begun already.

We should most of all recognize and admit Mrs. Eddy's own tolerance and love of those who fell short of demonstrating healing through spiritual means and give credence to her own written words on the matter of choice in healing methods.

The broadening of Mrs. Eddy's thought in the last decades of her life extended into the field of physical healing. She'd had enough opportunity to see that occasionally it didn't work. Healing wasn't always happening even in her own household. Dr. Gill wonders about this phenomenon, especially why Mrs. Eddy herself didn't heal the physical ailments that her staff encountered in the last decades of her life. Nobody explained why some people sickened and got worse and some died when they were around her. Shouldn't they have been raised, like the son of the widow of Nain?

Dr. Gill wrote: "To my mind, some kind of double think is certainly going on here, and it is common to all kinds of alternative healing. Claims are routinely made about cures effected in certain individuals, but silence shrouds other cases that failed to respond to treatment." (p. 403).

People in 1900 did not, and today, still do not want to break that silence about the failures. Exactly the problem of the brontosaurus in the living room.

Mrs. Eddy's answer went beyond the idea that she was no longer devoting herself to the calling of healing but was spending her time extending her scientific version of Christianity. She said then, and at other times, that it was very difficult to always demonstrate a high level of Christian healing. It could not happen in everyone at every moment, but was a journey towards spirituality, the work of years and days. That statement on her part is part of the realistic accommodation with human nature that can, and now should enable Christian Science to go forward through another century and beyond.

A new collection of Mrs. Eddy's heretofore unpublished writing, put out by the Christian Science Publishing Society, called

In My True Light: Collections from the Mary Baker Eddy Library for the Betterment of Humanity has an interesting piece of writing by the leader, circa 1901. Court cases and specific incidents among students caused her to write about surgical operations. Though it may seem surprising, surgery had seemingly always been allowed in the early days, although that has been forgotten in the twenty-first century. "Have the operation and use Christian Science for the healing," was her admonition for practitioners having to deal with certain realities.

Some students at that time wanted to know if they should allow anesthesia. It was one thing to have something repaired inside yourself, but wasn't ether medicine? Mrs. Eddy obviously didn't intend for anyone to suffer from the tortures of invasive surgery performed without anesthesia. That was ridiculous. Sometimes she must have sighed over these totally committed students. If a person decides he (or she) ought to have an operation, she wrote, and everybody around him is filling his and their own thought with the horrors of surgery with no pain relief, then the patient needs to just accede to the anesthesia. "Suffer this to be so now, for thus it becometh his humble follower to fulfil all righteousness—and take the ether. But the day is not far distant when this part of healing will be found more practical and safe through means of mind than matter" she wrote in that 1901 document. [A10407 p. 635.] Her own advice to students about this may apply to the larger field of allowing alternative means of healing if prayer isn't working: "Whatever change belongs to this century, or any epoch, we may safely submit to God, to common justice, individual rights and governmental usages," she also wrote.

During the last year of Mrs. Eddy's life, 1910, an article in *The Christian Science Journal*, the official publication of the church, apparently approved by her, was written by the editor of the magazine, Archibald McLellan. It is entitled "More Than a Cure-all." The premise of the article was that Christian Science was veering into the realm of sensational physical healing to the detriment of its theological principles. The faith system is not "a sort of family doctor," the editor warned. It is a path of Christian living. We can consider that a final word from the founding days, and good guidance for today. And WWJD? What would Jesus do?

He would, of course, heal the poor person dropping from life-threatening sickness, as He did when He walked the earth. His was that gift almost without fail. And what if the person couldn't get to him, try as he would, or didn't get healed, hampered by the same lack of faith and demonstration as Jesus felt in Nazareth or the disciples sometimes did on the road? Would he have allowed any option? Luke was a physician. We do not know if Jesus said to him, "Don't set that broken bone when you go out on the road. Rely only on prayer." Or did He approve of Luke's proving of his love of God by bringing healing balm and medical care to those in need? Surely He did. The Good Samaritan was commended by Jesus for offering first aid, the best medical care of the times, along with compassion and the love of God.

I am not arguing for any sort of radical revisionism—giving up the most basic tenets of the faith for easy answers. Christian Science is based on broad-based healing and that is its great gift to the world. Healing often results from spiritual growth and patience in prayer. Neither am I calling for combining medical treatment with Christian Science. Others combine medicine and prayer; Christian Science doesn't. I am calling for release of those who wish to seek healing after spiritual healing (which so often proves efficacious and superior) has not worked for them in the name of "common justice and individual rights." I am calling for social approval in Christian Science churches of alternative means of healing when necessary, of group sanction of individual choice, of the removal of the last and greatest of the hidden protocols which have tended to bind the Christian Science way of life for many—the consulting of physicians when necessary. Nobody leaves this life alive, as it has been said, of course, and people are dying all the time under medical care. Medical care is no panacea, but all must be given a fair shot at getting well.

And how will Christian Scientists know if they have life-threatening problems? They will know. And if they wish, they should feel free to have physical examinations from time to time without feeling a sense of betrayal of the group, themselves, or their God. I say announce and make it well known that physical examinations have good purposes in life.

Therefore, Christian Scientists must let it be known that theirs is a religion with arms wide open, that a newcomer can enter and learn and have fellowship and practice the understanding of God as All, without restrictions. Open the doors of the temple, and the all-knowing Christ triumphant will welcome and teach all mankind.

We can teach many, give much. Spiritual healing is the great gift Christian Science has to give to the rest of Christianity. A century of healing through prayer should be welcomed by those other denominations that follow Jesus and are increasingly interested in healing through prayer. Spiritual healing is a joy, a practical help, an ascending path. Christian Scientists need to fling wide the portals to all. Our great Truth should be known as a religion of living, not dying.

And could we all just get together again? Can we eliminate the splintering and agree on the central message of our faith without straining out gnats while we swallow camels?

Lastly, Christian Scientists must be their own best advocates in their communities. We know what is true through a lifetime of spiritual experience and can speak to other Christians about how a wide, non-restrictive view of healing can improve individuals, churches and communities—and the world and help fulfil the destiny of Christ's kingdom on earth. The old customs of letting others, hired and approved members of the Mother Church, speak for us has got to go. The traditional lectures will have clear and important roles in continuing to teach and inform, but ultimately our destiny and the future of our movement is in our own hands—out beyond Boston.

We have tongues ourselves and should visit the Presbyterians, Methodists and Catholics in our community at their

"Other ways, other paths" series—or whenever they call their investigations of other faiths—and speak out as brothers and sisters, as part of a rainbow of beliefs all of which center in Jesus Christ. Our average lay people should be part of college religion series, TV programs on prayer, conferences. Our emphasis is the theology of Christian Science—the ability to heal all of life through spiritual living and the conquering of sin. We need an intensive campaign to spread the total commitment news we believe in. We need to actively court the press with the message of new ideas for a new time, to have respected people in the local churches schedule lunches with opinion makers, make friends, spread the word. There has been good press lately about all sorts of spiritually-centered life paths, and Christian Science has had positive coverage in Protestant denominational, feminist and Catholic publications. We need to build on that.

And while still retaining the integrity of our own belief system, that established with us and for us by an inspired spiritual leader almost one-hundred fifty years ago, we need to respect and cooperate with the central Protestant tradition from which we emerged. Moving towards fuller fellowship with all Christians to the greatest extent possible is a desired goal which will bring results in general understanding of our way of life and its ability to contribute to Christian thought.

After many years of defining the differences between Christian Science and other Protestant denominations, of drawing sharp lines—of using a language which was different from theirs and outlining doctrinal interpretations that differed—Mrs. Eddy herself in the last ten or fifteen years of her life began to reach out to traditional Protestant denominations, to explain her discovery in terms of typical Protestant values.

She moved to the center instead of staying on the fringes. She began to realize that it would be from the ranks of traditional Protestantism that she must draw adherents and that to agree again with them she must broaden the church's outreach, understand the stern demands her religion had made on people and reduce them somewhat.

One need only look at the evolution of her spiritual interpretation of the Lord's Prayer to its final edition to see how the last decade of her life was devoted to mellowing, reorienting herself and her religion to the larger sphere of Christianity. Earlier versions do not mention grace or heaven, traditional Christian terms.

In the real world of twenty-first century journalism, media will continue to seek out disgruntled Christian Scientists whenever any new criticism surfaces and these folk will write articles about their sad upbringings and personal experiences, venting their own feelings, an example of the few speaking for the great many in the name of "Truth."

Those of us who do not feel we are the stuporous victims of thought-control, aimlessly following a demented old lady's ravings, but instead the thoughtful followers of a faith system we believe works for spiritual growth need to get honest and go into our communities. What we do, what we believe, we think serves ourselves, our community and Christ well and we need to spread that word.

Christianity is a rainbow and it is also a river, now again the fastest growing religion in the world. Through two thousand years various streams have fed this river. The power and ecclesiastical system of the early church deepened the channels of the river so it spread around the world, the monastic tradition fed its introspective current. The Reformation stirred and cleared the waters. Today evangelical Christianity, Vatican II Catholicism, with a new emphasis on the Scriptures, ecumenism and the community church movement of the Protestants, Mormonism with its emphasis on the family, all swell the central stream. All preach the validity of a life of salvation, meaning and eternal destiny lived through Jesus the Christ. Christian Science adds its valid and important stream of healing and reliance on God as All. We all as Christians can benefit from understanding the richness of the variety of currents now in the central river, but Christian Scientists must stir and clarify their own stream before that can happen.

I believe the time will come when the powers of mind and spirit will be fully understood and all people will heal themselves from all sin, disease, and death, through the power of the creative intelligence which rules the universe.

But until that time comes, we must live with compassion, tolerance, and practicality.

These young people who are taking over the business meetings in key Christian Science churches and demanding to be heard about change are destined to have their way. If they have it, they may be able to bring a very valuable and vital tradition of Christianity into the future.

This is one brontosaurus—the church's tarnished reputation and misunderstood mission—which everyone in the Christian Science movement will be glad to send to extinction.

The future can be as bright as we, with God's help, make it.